Wingin' It

Wingin' It

The Art of
Personal Leadership

EQ at Work

Don Wohlenhaus

1998
Galde Press, Inc.
PO Box 460, Lakeville, Minnesota 55044–0460, U.S.A.

Wingin' It
© Copyright 1998 by Don Wohlenhaus

First Edition
First Printing, 1998

Library of Congress Cataloging-in-Publication Data
   Wohlenhaus, Don.
      Wingin' it : the art of personal leadership / Don
      Wohlenhaus.
         p.   cm.
      ISBN 1–880090–60–0 (pbk.)
         1. Psychology, Industrial.   2. Success in business—
   Psychological aspects.   3. Emotions and cognition.
   4. Interpersonal relations.   I. Title.
   HF5548.8.W595   1998
   158.7—dc21   97–52275
                                                          CIP

Galde Press, Inc.
PO Box 460
Lakeville, Minnesota 55044–0460

To all who are wingin' it
and for all who should

Contents

Acknowledgements

When I close my eyes and think about all the people who have nurtured me, inspired me, and who brought me to this point in my life, I see a parade of faces and smiles. First I wish to acknowledge my partner for over thirty years, my wife, Nell, whose best feature is being happy when she has no good reason to feel that way.

I see Ken Light, who saw in me a vast potential. I see Don Schiel who taught me that optimism is a learned emotion. Larry Haeg, Sr., is in the line too; he defined what good radio was all about, and his legacy still lives on today at WCCO. I see Richard F. McCarthy, who showed me why values in action are the only way to build intimate, long-term relationships. Freddy Boos is there; he taught me what persistence and vision are all about. I see my hero, Harry Stanius, who taught me why integrity in golf would always serve me well in life.

Joe Bailey is the one who put me in touch with my dark side and taught me how to forgive myself when I do dumb things. George Pransky is there; he taught me and continues to teach me emotional intelligence. I recognize Larry Haeg, Jr., who not only is my role model of someone with both high emotional and intellectual intelligence, but has been an indispensable sounding board and expert on writing for this project. His comments and corrections on the various drafts of this book have been invaluable. I thank him for writing the foreword to this book.

Mark Ronnei shows up as my best example of why the world loves someone of solid character. I see Jim Akervik, Brad Smith, John Thedinga, and Gary Hammer in line, and I acknowledge what they've taught me about long-term client relationships. I see Cher Johnson, whose strategies on dealing with people inspired me to write this book. I recognize Blair Witt, Ginger Sisco, Kevin Moore, Dave Haeg, and Deb Stregge, who all contributed their time and efforts to improve the book's relevance, organization, and readability.

I see my mother, Rose, and I acknowledge that she always believed in me. I see my kids, Dave, Deb, and Steve, who have forced me to grow in spite of myself.

Finally, I acknowledge Miles B. Canning, my collaborator and editor, who helped me to clarify and organize my own thinking. Miles is one of the best examples of someone who's wingin' it most successfully.

—DONALD LEE WOHLENHAUS

Buffalo, Minnesota
December 15, 1996

Foreword

Thirty-two years ago—after my sophomore year in college—my father suggested I spend the summer working at a radio station in Brainerd, Minnesota. It seemed like a good idea. I was enchanted with radio—and so off I went. What I got a taste of that summer was not so much the radio business but a firsthand lesson in entrepreneurism.

My mentor was the station manager, a twenty-nine-year-old dynamo named Donald Lee Wohlenhaus. Don not only managed the station, but he sold time and had his own daily three-hour air shift. In short, he did everything, and he did it with gusto. To say that Don was energetic is understating it a bit. He race-walked to client calls, creating his own private jet stream. He ate fast. He talked fast. He could move around the room while seated. He even ran between shots on the golf course. I distinctly remember the rattle of his clubs in his bag as he lumbered past me down the fairway. "Come on, Haeg, get a move on!" he would yell.

I also noticed Don knew how to connect with people. He knew how to find a person's wavelength. He listened. He had empathy. By the time the summer was over I was exhausted just trying to keep up with him and more than a little relieved to return to campus. But I had made a careful mental note of what I had seen and heard—here was a firsthand example of someone who worked awfully hard for what he earned. My father, Larry Haeg, Sr., created one of the nation's most listened-to radio stations, WCCO. He had preached to me many times that nothing comes without hard effort, taking some risks, determination. Well, here was a real-life example. Although we went our separate ways after that summer of '64, we always stayed in touch; we knew each other's families, we were both in radio, and my father was one of Don's mentors.

So here we are, thirty-two years later, and Don has asked me to write a few words for his foreword. I won't repeat what's in the book. You can read that for yourself. What I can do first is to tell you a little about Don, so you can appreciate the experience and wisdom he brings to his work today, and second, I can tell you what effect he's had on me.

First, about Don. The voice you hear in the book is the voice of someone who is, very simply, self-made. He was born in 1935 at the very bottom of the Depression in the very midst of the Dust Bowl—in a little tumbleweed town called Davenport, Oklahoma, midway between Tulsa and Oklahoma City. His father sharecropped wheat. Like Steinbeck's Joad family in *The Grapes of Wrath,* they packed up their belongings and headed for California, where they found work in the vineyards near Fresno. Four years later, Don's father left the family. Don moved with his mother to the Bay Area, where she worked during World War Two as a riveter at the Kaiser Shipyards, and Don rode the cable cars to school.

In 1945, she married a farmer from Minnesota, and they drove back across the plains to a town called Trimont in the southwestern part of the state, living on a farm with no indoor plumbing and no electricity. Don milked the cows, shoveled manure, went to a one-room schoolhouse, and was graduated from Windom High School. After three years in the Air Force and a brief period at Brown Institute in the Twin Cities, he began a twenty-five-year career in sales, first with P. Lorillard, then Fuller Laboratories, and then to sales, management and ownership positions with radio stations throughout Minnesota.

Today, as a consultant, a motivator, and a counselor, dozens of businesses across the state seek him out for guidance as technology continues to revolutionize the nature and meaning of "work" and redefines the shape of corporations. So, if you're considering the next move in your career (or careers), or if you're running a business that's being tossed around by change, I ask you—who would you rather have on your side? A graduate of an Ivy League school, long on academic pedigree, or a man with much more than a college education? Don has been a highly successful salesman, corporate executive, business owner, and a much sought after independent business consultant for over three decades.

Second, what has Don done for me? Well, I can best answer that by recalling Richard Dreyfuss in the movie *Mr. Holland's Opus*. It is the story of three decades in the life of a high school music teacher who inspires his students not just to play the notes on the page but to feel the spirit, the energy, the rhythm of the music itself. In one memorable scene, Mr. Holland takes the page of notes away from a frustrated, young clarinet player and tells her to play with feeling, not from notes. "Stranger on the Shore" never sounded more beautiful on the clarinet.

Well, that's what Don Wohlenhaus taught me and thousands of others: don't look to institutions for all the answers, take charge of your life, follow your inner voice, measure your options prudently, and take some risks. It's certainly more challenging than playing someone else's notes, and in the end, it's a lot more rewarding.

So this unique book is, if you will, Mr. Wohlenhaus' Opus. I highly recommend it.

Thank you, Mr. Wohlenhaus.

—LARRY HAEG, JR.

Vice President, Corporate Communications
Norwest Corporation
December 1, 1996

Introduction

I believe the American work force is on the brink of an age of productivity that will eclipse the agrarian, industrial, and information ages. It will be led by individuals who have a tradition of personal freedoms and who are confident of their own destiny. Individual growth and corporate success will multiply in a system that encourages employee investment. The changes in the way we work will enrich more lives than ever in the history of mankind.

True to our American heritage and our most common image to foreigners, Americans are doers. We Yankees are sometimes criticized but often admired for our quick decision making and decisive action. These are the very traits that allow us to successfully compete in a world which is changing rapidly. We Americans are able to make quick decisions because of our depth of positive cultural values. We want to make quick decisions because we are impatient for immediate gratification. We make good, quick decisions because we take responsibility for our decisions. We grow and learn because, as individuals, we possess both the opportunity to achieve and the willingness to be accountable for our decisions. Our abilities to react, to be flexible, and to make the most of our opportunities have brought us to our present leadership position.

This is not to say these changes are easy to make and that every person who works would welcome self-development. Some individuals have a hard time making quick decisions, and some people refuse even to try. In some cases the sense of urgency just does not exist, or perhaps the opportunity to make one's own decisions does not exist. In other cases no accountability for decision making is demanded. Some managers have hoarded all the authority and power of making decisions for themselves. Some managers have been willing to accept the decision making role by default as part of their care-taking role. But today, no business can afford to support people who have to be told what to do. We cannot afford the extra bodies on the payroll, and we cannot afford the time it takes to communicate up and down the line. With labor being often the most expensive cost for a business, higher individual productivity can give a business significant competitive advantages.

Companies with productivity problems often can trace these problems back to their own work force and to the organizational structures that govern how work is done. Good people working in a caretaking or negative situation can find themselves discouraged and can feel trapped. Some companies have developed a kind of employee dependence on management. When this happens, people may lose ambition, creativity, and an individual work ethic. The twin curses of dependence and entitlement make some people so dull that they won't make any of their own decisions because they're either intimidated or apathetic. It doesn't have to be this way; we can change.

In today's global, high-tech, information-laden marketplace, quick and high-quality decision making at every level is not just a competitive advantage in business, but a survival skill. Some encouragement for us to change comes from without. The demands of the marketplace may require us to learn new skills, for instance. Employees who do not control what they do at work have become expendable. And some encouragement for us to change comes from within and consists of our self-motivating needs for growth and meaning in our work lives. My consulting practice is dedicated to helping all individuals make quicker and better decisions so that their asset value and the productivity they bring to the company will both increase. The simple steps I urge you to take in this book will lead you toward more personal leadership, more positive relationships in your life, and more productivity in whatever you choose to do.

Throughout this book I'm addressing different individuals in different roles, but all with the same advice. Whether you are a manager, an employee, a business owner, or a volunteer, my message to you is to be all you can be, especially in your work role. Some people insist that a book has to be written for one or the other audience, as if readers who are in management require different kinds of information from other readers. I don't think so. In all of our lives we play all of these roles, and we can learn from the perspectives of others.

This is a serious book about personal power, and it's a positive book with a hopeful message. It's a business-oriented book because it's about the work we all do, but I believe nonprofits, government organizations, and millions of people who do not get paid for their work will find helpful insights here. The "you" I address here is the same you regardless of what your current work role may be; your path toward self-actualization, (and yours and yours), begins and ends with you.

This book begins with a focus on your individual potential. At some point we all have to make decisions and act in order to achieve the fulfillment, growth, and self-satisfaction we all say we want from our work and our lives; this book will help you get rid of past barriers to action and encourage you to create a dynamic work life for yourself, regardless of where you work or what you do. This is how to influence the culture in which you work—from the inside out. The first step is to achieve a heightened level of self-understanding. Self-understanding includes an awareness of your values and a realization of your potential for greatness. Your "EQ" or "emotional intelligence" or "self-understanding" is a measure of how much self-control you are willing and able to exert in order to get what you want. I call this personal leadership.

Most chapters in this book promote effective ways of relating to other people. Most decision making in business today is influenced by or tries to influence other people: customers, suppliers, co-workers, or people above or below you on the organizational chart. Over forty years of working in corporate America has convinced me that building intimate working relationships is what makes working worthwhile. Relationships give meaning and value to what we do for at least a third of our lives, half our waking hours. If your relationships with co-workers, customers, or suppliers aren't positive, aren't supportive and invigorating for you, either change your work or change your attitude. Having humility and compassion for others, and building intimacy in relationships are pre-requisites to relating to other people effectively, but very few people understand their significance.

If your market or business is changing, and you intend to continue to participate, you may have to change your role or even think differently than you do now. You will embrace change if you are in control. Companies are using these ideas right now without wholesale reorganizations, without expensive implementation campaigns, and with-out fear of failure. After all, real change occurs one indi-vidual at a time, one relationship at a time. The time for positive change is now.

I'm reluctant, but my editor insists I tell you a bit about myself in this introduction since so much of this book is my opinion and you have a right to know on what basis I presume to know anything. Since I identify the people I use as examples in this book by what they do and to prove a point, I reveal something about their interaction with people or the creative ways they build relationships, I'll do the same with myself.

In my fifties I discovered that achieving career successes such as being a top salesperson, or having the titles of vice president of sales and marketing or general manager, or even owning radio stations were not enough for me. I have been and done these things. My career successes resulted from hard work and the application of skills I've been lucky to possess, but these achievements didn't satisfy me. Something was missing in my life, and it had to do with my own growth and development as a person. I have learned the real doers, the people who know who they are, where they're going, and who enjoy their lives are wingin' it. When I urge you to raise your emotional intelligence in order to make better quick decisions, I am speaking from my own experience.

In 1983, a close friend and I conceived of a news network that would unite all of greater Minnesota with quality news, sports, and weather programming, and we started the Minnesota News Network (MNN). In 1990, I was asked to become the President of the Network, which now had seventy commercial radio stations in Minnesota. I discovered the real value of relationship building, humility, compassion, and intimacy during the next five years, for I began to truly integrate my work life and my personal life. In December of 1994, I left MNN to devote full time to my consulting business and to work as a teacher, motivator, and facilitator for other people's personal growth.

Much of my appreciation for personal growth and development is relatively new to me. As far as my own growth and development, I believe I've learned more in the past five years than I learned in the previous thirty-five years I spent succeeding in business. This growth for me has not been the result of any particular religious experience or cataclysmic event or dramatic discovery, and anyone can choose to do what I've done. I have worked at it, but it has not been a fanatic quest or some painful ritual of self-denial. In fact, as I tell my clients, personal growth and development is a long road, it's a lifelong process, and the important thing is to get on the right road, right now.

I am certainly humbled by my aged wisdom, but I'm also more confident and sure of myself than I've ever been. This is the essential paradox of people I observe who are wingin' it. They are calm, self-satisfied, and sure of themselves, yet they can make good decisions quickly, even under fire. They are risk takers and careful at the same time. I know my capacity for making good judgments is heightened by my emotional maturity and by my conscious efforts at self-control.

Management advice which claims to instantly fix personnel problems has never been attractive to me because it doesn't seem to work for long (or at all). Examining our attitudes about work and understanding what motivates us are more valuable. I'm writing this book to proclaim how important my friends and relationships have been in my life, and I want to share their lessons to me with a wider audience. I want others to experience the excitement, the power, and the rewards of being the best they can be. This book shows you how to manage your own destiny and build relationships that help you grow. When you are growing and learning, you are more productive, and any enterprise that includes you will prosper.

EQ Is Personal Leadership

➤ **We can choose the thoughts** we will embrace and act upon; we become more emotionally intelligent to the degree we practice personal leadership.

➤ **Knowing the priority of our own values** enables us to choose our best course of action more quickly and with more self-confidence; this is how emotional intelligence translates into being productive.

➤ **Knowing the priorities of our company's values** and using our emotional intelligence enable us to make decisions with others more quickly that are in the best interests of the company.

Chapter One
EQ Is Personal Leadership

Y EARS AGO I WAS BROWSING in the psychology section at B. Dalton when I came across a book titled *The Serenity Principle,* by Joe Bailey, Ph.D. Joe is a psychologist in St. Paul, Minnesota, not far from where I live. I met Joe, and he shared with me the ideas and concepts that are the foundation for his book. They come from the psychology of mind (POM), a contemporary branch of behavioral psychology. He introduced me to one of his mentors, George Pransky, Ph.D. George is a prolific author of audio- and videotapes as well as books and articles. He wrote *The Relationship Handbook*, which is based on the psychology of mind principles.

I visited George and his wife, Linda, both psychologists, at their home and work center in La Conner, Washington, a small fishing village north of Seattle. George has

a common-sense approach in sharing the possibilities of
how to feel you are in control of your life. When he shares
his ideas with you, in a non-clinical manner, they make
sense. The mind, thought, and consciousness are the keys
to our internal capacity to solve our own problems.

"Our circumstances and how we view or respond to
our circumstances are two different things," Dr. Pransky
stated. He maintained that we can choose which thoughts
we will embrace, and that this choice can change our circumstances for the better. To understand the mind, we
need to see it as the source of our emotions and our perceptions. Thought creates images in our heads, and consciousness is the faculty, or power, that makes these images
appear real to our senses. Mind and consciousness are
both constants; the only variable is thought.

Whatever we experience as "our life" is determined by
how we think. This is why two people can be in the same
circumstances and have totally different perceptions. Self-
determination, or choosing how we think about our circumstances, is the foundation of the American Dream. I
can remember my high school English teacher Frances
Johnson telling me this many years ago.

Why should you be concerned about your thinking?
Today the majority of us have lost a sense of security, that
trust and belief we once had that a company or organization would give us the guarantee of a job. We are experiencing the most significant changes in the history of our
country regarding jobs and careers. It's my observation

that work has replaced jobs in our culture. These changes we are experiencing are impacting everyone, including executives, managers, and supervisors, and no job will escape its implications. How we think, how we respond to circumstances, and how we engineer ourselves to increase our asset value are the fundamental issues in all of our work lives.

In my consulting practice the people I see who are most successful in dealing with rapid change are those who are wingin' it; they make quick decisions that turn out to be good decisions. In deciding to write a book that would help people to be successful in this mode of decision making, I'm aware that many people are uncomfortable with being required to make quick decisions. They'd rather take more time. I understand this desire. But slowness in decision making is not an asset in business today. Successful business owners and people who are still employed share this one ability: they're wingin' it.

They make quick decisions and have a sure, positive attitude about taking action. They are not frantic under pressure. They are flexible yet dependable. They command respect and loyalty by their actions, not by their job titles. To have the confidence these people have, you must understand your moods and manage your own behavior. You must have self-control, in other words, emotional intelligence. Having a purpose or fulfilling a meaningful, personal expectation is also part of this confidence.

Values are coming back in vogue in business circles today. More individuals are asking, "What are my priorities, what's my purpose?"

Since some sort of value judgments are required for all decisions, interest in clarifying one's own values should be the first step in making faster decisions. People who have clearly defined their own values are able to look at a company's values and see where there are matches. When they can share some values with the company, working with other people becomes easier and more productive. When one's own values can be practiced at work, work itself becomes more fulfilling by definition.

All organizations, just like all people, have sets of values upon which they act. Although it may not be necessary to have perfect matches between what the company believes and what individuals believe, it is necessary for individuals to understand what the company stands for. For example, it is essential for all individuals to know values the company believes are most important when it comes to making decisions. By writing down and prioritizing our own values as well as participating in this same exercise in our workplace, we come to understand ourselves better, and most of all we discover we are much more than we thought we were. This is a freeing insight.

Those who are wingin' it use their common sense more than pat solutions to problems. Each of us has an inborn capacity for common sense, which is a different kind of intelligence than is typically measured with an IQ test or with letter grades. Dr. Peter Salovey, from Yale University, and Dr. John Mayer from University of New Hampshire coined the term, "emotional intelligence" around 1990. According to an article titled "The EQ Factor," by Nancy Gibbs in the October 2, 1995, cover story in *Time* magazine, their description of the term includes "understanding one's feelings," "having empathy for the feelings of others," and "the regulation of emotion in a way that enhances living."

"EQ"—A Different Kind of Smartness

The contemporary book *Emotional Intelligence* by Daniel Goleman, Ph.D. (Bantam, 1995), popularizes the idea that EQ is a different kind of smartness. He writes:

Emotional intelligence includes self-awareness and impulse control, persistence, zeal and self-motivation, empathy and social deftness. These are the qualities that mark people who excel in real life: whose intimate relationships flourish, who are stars in the workplace. These are also the hallmarks of self-discipline, of altruism and compassion—basic capacities needed if our society is to thrive.

Mental intelligence is often measured by the "IQ" or intelligence test. The measure is expressed as a number on a scale from low to high. The comparison between "IQ" and "EQ" stops with the conceptual naming of different facets of what we call intelligence. All sorts of intelligences influence how we communicate, relate, and respond to our environment. When we see EQ in action, we see it as maturity, or we refer to it as sound judgment, or just plain savvy. "EQ" and "emotional intelligence" are used interchangeably to describe factors that apparently influence all of our behavior. There really is no test like the Stanford Binet test of intelligence which renders the Intelligence Quotient score, shortened to "IQ." As far as I know, there is no "Emotional Quotient" or comparable test to arrive at a score.

What the contemporary writers are talking about are factors other than those typically measured by an IQ test that influence behavior. The discoveries in current research demonstrate that success in business and, more broadly, in life has much more to do with emotional intelligence, and perhaps much less to do with intellectual intelligence than previously known. That emotions are powerful motivators and that our feelings can influence our behavior aren't new insights. But acknowledging feelings and emotions in the workplace is not a common practice in the business world. But to me, our ability to understand our emotions and interact constructively with others is essential to our success in business or anywhere else.

Those who are wingin' it have a high EQ. They have a positive perspective on life, especially their work. They have practical, "gut level" wisdom that helps them understand how life works. They have optimism, unconditional self-esteem, humility, compassion, and the ability to work with intensity. All these are learned behaviors that any of us can acquire.

How We Become Emotionally Intelligent

Negative, self-defeating thoughts are as influential in forming your personality as are positive thoughts. Low emotional intelligence is a result of your inability to recognize or change self-defeating, counter-productive thoughts. You can learn a habit of insecurity, and often you can find others to take care of you, which reinforces a dependent view of life. On the other hand, once you choose to be more productive, to grow, learn new habits, and control your own life, your emotional intelligence begins to soar. People with high emotional intelligence are good at wingin' it because they take responsibility for their decisions, they're invested in the consequences of their decisions, and they understand what their contribution means to others.

Motivational authors and speakers have preached this concept for many years. They call it the power of positive thinking or prosperity consciousness or, simply, will power. Most people agree with the concepts but don't consciously control their thoughts unless a crisis happens. In distress, people can be more open to changing their thoughts. They look for ways out of their psychological pain. But what George Pransky and the others advocate is an internalized, disciplined way of living that connects our thoughts to feelings and directs us to act in ways consistent with our positive values.

It's wonderful news that we can liberate the mind from self-defeating, negative thought patterns anytime we wish. But the psychology-of-mind psychologists encourage us to invest time and energy to develop our minds and control our destinies all the time, not just when we seem to be failing. The potential for practically influencing individual growth and development is what's so exciting about these ideas.

Raising our emotional intelligence levels empowers us to be more self-directed. Dr. Pransky was formerly a more traditional psychologist and would have his patients talking about all their troubles, disappointments, and failures in his therapy sessions. He came to believe this psychoanalytical process was self-defeating. He began applying psychology of mind in his professional practice. Other psychologists were using these concepts, writing about them, and reporting successful therapeutic results. The experts were clearly demonstrating the efficacy of self-determination or rational motive therapy as a powerful basis for individual growth. If people believe what happens to them is beyond their control, they will not take responsibility for what happens to them. Just the opposite results from acknowledging our power to choose our next thought. We take responsibility. We move forward. We learn. This is personal leadership.

Our Thoughts and Our Actions

You can choose the thoughts you think are best for you, and then you can make a decision to act on those thoughts. You also have a choice of not acting on your thoughts. We all can imagine all sorts of things we don't act on. We can experience anger at someone without physically assaulting the person. We can admire an object without stealing it. Our sense of values helps us manage our thoughts, and our thoughts determine our actions.

What we do act on is important because it reinforces our values and shows the world who we are. What we do is always a choice we have made, and this is where the psychology-of-mind practitioners depart from other psychologists. The individual always has a choice as to what actions he or she will take. Even in the midst of oppressive or threatening coercion, the individual has a choice. Even with a history of making bad choices, the individual can change his or her behavior by changing his or her thinking. We can make better decisions by the conscious application of our will.

The Receiver Thought Mode

We need to get away from analytical thinking. We need to get away from trying to figure everything out and the need to have an answer for everything. Clear your mind. "Go with your innate mental health," says Joe Bailey. He asserts children all have innate mental health because they don't analyze or judge what they do.

He says, "If you doubt what I'm telling you, please spend some time with a two-, three-, or four-year-old. Up until about age four you find that kids have no self-image; they don't adopt alter egos." In this context both self-image and ego are used to describe negative self-perceptions that are put on. Young children are usually very spontaneous and genuine, and they don't try to play roles. They basically have good self-esteem. They have confidence. They don't mind being confrontational. If you say no to them, they kind of roll with the punch. They get mad at you, but they don't stay that way very long. You look out the window and you see a couple kids fighting and two minutes later they're hugging one another.

Alan Flood, author of *Management By Inspiration*, insists that it is our attempts to adopt phony self-images that lead to low self-esteem and failures to communicate with others on a genuine, sincere level. The shoulds and superficial stereotypes we try to adopt are unproductive and destructive. One friend of mine refers to our tendencies to put on airs as "inner-kill," or the art of dying without knowing it. I know that those successful people I see in leadership positions have no self-image. They are the same people off the job and on the job. They don't put on airs, pretend to be someone else, or care about appearances. They're consistent, aligned, predictable.

How do you know if you're wingin' it? Your first clue will be a feeling of ease and contentment. Feelings of self-assurance, self-worth and optimism should follow. Next you'll have strong feelings of humility and compassion. You'll find your focus is on changing yourself rather than changing others. Then you'll start getting lucky.

This optimistic perspective that praises the virtues of common sense and high emotional intelligence is potentially available to everyone at all times. It's hard to teach; most likely, it can only be learned. To be successful at wingin' it, try to stay in the receiver mode as often as possible.

I have applied these concepts to my own life, and I know they're sound. I have committed myself to trust my own values. I have developed a confidence in my own power by accepting who I am. I encounter the world with an eagerness to learn what I don't know. At home, in my consulting work, and socially, I try to have compassion for others and establish intimate relationships. When I see others using these ideas and being successful, I am further convinced of their efficacy. Adam Martinez is a chemical health specialist who works for a client of mine, and he's as good an example as any of how the psychology of mind principles can be applied on the job.

Adam's Story

Adam has had his trials and tribulations in life, culminating in a successful third drug treatment and a career in drug counseling. His counseling approach is different from the more traditional twelve-step or Alcoholics Anonymous methodology. The twelve-step approach typically encourages participants to talk about all the bad things that have happened in their lives, all the horror stories or "drunkalogues." AA members are helped to relate these disasters to the use of their drug of choice, and to further study their disease. The recovery process includes submitting to a higher power, however you describe that power, making amends or atoning for past behavior, and committing to abstain daily.

When he participated in these groups, Adam observed that all the talk about the past would make everybody's spirits and moods go down. Misery loved company, and he saw everyone feeling bad, guilty, and powerless. Invariably someone would start crying because the pain was so bad. He reasoned that such emphasis on the past was not warranted. Change is what his clients wanted, and they couldn't change their pasts by any amount of analyzing. Having studied the psychology of mind, he started using the self-affirming, decision-making concepts with his patients at the treatment center where he worked.

He found out he could get extraordinary results with a more positive approach when these individuals became more aware of their abilities to choose their thoughts and behavior. He helps build people's confidence and self-esteem by helping them live in the moment. "You've got a great mind; what are you focused on right now? What are you doing now? What are you thinking now? What are your feelings now? What direction would you like to go today?" He won't let his clients dwell in the past because he thinks that doesn't help at all.

He takes every opportunity to help other people get into self-understanding. He radiates warmth and self-confidence, and he has a wonderful ability to deal with people. It's amazing how many job offers he's received because his clients are moving on, but he says he's not interested in changing jobs. "Nothing can give you the feeling of watching another human being go to a higher level of self-understanding. When I see a person developing compassion for other people, I see a wonderful person coming alive. I see no limits to what they can do. This is what I want to see. This is what I want to do."

I am inspired by Adam, Dr. Pransky, and many other practitioners. I see how increasing your emotional intelligence can enhance the lives of working people and the companies in which they work. As a business consultant, anything which can help people be more productive is of great interest to me. I am convinced that strong, confident, self-reliant individuals will contribute more to an enterprise. Companies should invest in their people not only because it's the ethical thing to do, but also because it is more profitable to do so. This book is dedicated to the idea that all people can consciously focus on learning, growing, and increasing their competencies and that all companies will ultimately benefit from their increased productivity.

Try taking the self-assessment below. You'll get a good idea of some characteristics which equate to a high EQ and that I feel contribute toward an ability to make better quick decisions. See where you stand by tallying your score after answering the following statements:

Wingin' It Self-Assessment

Answer "Yes" or "No" to the following statements

	YES	NO
1. I value internal security more than external security.	___	___
2. I listen for feeling more than content.	___	___
3. My thoughts dictate my emotions.	___	___
4. I am usually more humble about myself than I am arrogant.	___	___
5. I know I can always choose to change.	___	___
6. I don't try to change other people.	___	___
7. I work with intensity rather than effort.	___	___
8. I am content in my personal and work lives.	___	___
9. Learning is a competitive advantage.	___	___
10. I develop intimate working relationships.	___	___
11. I have high expectations for myself, and I exceed them most of the time.	___	___

	YES	NO
12. In problem solving I use the receiver mode more than the computer mode of decision making.	___	___
13. I care for rather than caretake other people at work.	___	___
14. I link my thoughts with my feelings and purpose.	___	___
15. I rely on my common sense most of the time.	___	___
16. I feel comfortable with risk.	___	___
17. Investment and commitment pay off.	___	___
18. Delayed gratification is usually worth the wait.	___	___
19. I understand everyone has moods, and I accommodate my own moods.	___	___
20. I feel compassion more than sympathy for people's troubles.	___	___

This is only a conceptual tool; no mathematics are involved in tallying up your results. Score a bull's eye for every affirmative response you've made, and read on to discover specifically what I mean by these ideas. The assessment is a way to contrast various ways of approaching life, with the positive answers above comprising assets for you in your ability to make better quick decisions, and with answers in the negative comprising liabilities or barriers to being able to improvise successfully. All of us can place ourselves somewhere on this continuum; I believe the closer you are to the affirmative side, the more flexible, creative, and effective you will be in making decisions, especially under pressure.

Your Assets

➤ **Knowledge alone can't substitute for wisdom.**
Today it's impossible to possess all the knowledge
needed for future decision making. Being able to
learn is your greatest asset.

➤ **If you are true to your values,** and you grow, learn,
and do work the best you can, you need not be particularly concerned about what you do.

➤ **Taking an inventory of your values** lets you know
what the most important areas in your life are—it's
your guidebook to decision making.

Chapter Two
Your Assets

YEARS AGO TEACHERS used to teach values in school. They graded you on all kinds of values. I remember getting a score on punctuality, deportment, attitude, respect, and so forth. In the last thirty years we've gotten away from that. Your real asset value is what's in your character, your willingness and ability to learn, and your emotional intelligence.

Whether it's because of negative messages via the media, or because parents and teachers are too busy to be involved in teaching good values, or because of the idea that positive values don't need to be taught, positive values seem scarce with a lot of young people today. Ask some young people what kind of things they value, and they'll tell you money. They'll talk about clothes and cars and things. They'll tell you a that good job means they've made it, that they feel entitled. Today many young people, and lots of older people, too, don't make good decisions because they don't know on what criteria they should base their decisions.

People who are able to function at high levels prepare themselves. They decide what is most important for themselves; they prioritize. To have, you must first become, and by the process of becoming you acquire values. It's discipline. It's the work of learning a craft, a skill, or a body of knowledge that you can master. Nurturing families engender good values, but many people who did not have healthy families have still acquired good values. Many people put in years of learning through the triumphs and tragedies of various relationships with other people before they become the kind of people they can respect. Learning about the world in school or on the job is not a matter of mere information—that would be easy. Wisdom and self-confidence require much more than information and work experience.

The Limited Value of Knowledge

A problem with the messages of the past fifty years is that "knowledge" is seen as the only ticket to ride. We were all told that all we needed was knowledge. Kids have expectations that if they get the good grades and learn the material, the world's their oyster. But this isn't true. You need more than knowledge. You need street experience, and you need to develop judgment or common sense to make good decisions. You put solid knowledge and good street-wise experience together and you have people who are real good at wingin' it.

Young people today were told if they had the knowledge, if they got the grades, and if they graduated from college, then a job would be waiting for them. They were told if they disciplined themselves to go to school, the $50,000 to $60,000-a-year job, the big bucks, the bonus would follow. But this is not true. And many young people are severely disillusioned. You have to make your own job, and usually you need some help from whatever network or friends, family, and mentors you've accumulated through your relationships. A personal example can help illustrate this idea that values are learned through relationships, not through academic study.

Back in the early sixties I really wanted to break into the radio world. WCCO 830 (or 'CCO to locals) was the biggest thing in radio at that time, so I got to know people there like Charlie Boone, Roger Erickson, Howard Viken, Joyce Lamont, and Bob DeHaven. I also got to know Larry Haeg, Sr., the general manager, who would become my mentor a couple of years later. One of his very successful salesmen was Ken Light.

He and I hit it off very well. He's the one who gave me the confidence to move to Brainerd, Minnesota, back in 1962, when I was all of twenty-seven years old, and start a radio station from scratch. Ken was one of those guys who had that innate ability to look at you and say, "Yes you can!"

"But Ken, I've never been on the air, I've never run a radio station, what do I do?"

He said "You'll have to do whatever, because I won't be up there. You'll have to pick out the site for the radio station, and you'll have to hire the people for the radio station. You're going to have to be intimately involved in deciding the programming of the radio station, and you probably will have to work on the air because we won't be able to afford a lot of anything for a while!"

He continued with this irresistible sales pitch: "You'll have to be the manager, the number one salesman, and the program director. You're going to have to do everything for a while." Then he said, "Look at it this way, you'll get your Masters in radio, maybe even your Ph.D. And I will support you. I will back you in that endeavor because you can do it."

With the exponential explosion of knowledge in the information age, it is literally impossible for anyone to have all the knowledge that will be required in the future to make sound judgments. Many young people today go to college, get a degree in something, and think this degree is what they're going to do, right? I learned early on that you never know exactly what you're going to be, you never know what you're going to do. If you're eighteen years old today, you can expect to have at least seven career changes before you're thirty. There is no linear line.

If you're fortunate enough, maybe you'll meet four or five people who will have a most dramatic impact on your life because they believe in you. Perhaps you need to acknowledge a few mentors already. These people are very good at what they do, and they want you to be successful. Ken Light wanted me to be successful, and I knew it. He told me, I believed him, and I rose to his expectations not because I just wanted some title like general manager, but because he gave me the confidence that with all the challenges and drawbacks, I could make it work.

If there is no magic path, no pat formula, no ticket to ride, academic or otherwise, what are you left with? Know yourself. Become self-reliant. Choose to grow and learn to be the best at what you do, which is in itself a value I try to live and teach others. If you are true to your values, and you grow, learn, and do work the best you can, you need not be particularly concerned about what you do.

The Self-Esteem Trap

You don't have to think well of yourself to have self-esteem. On the contrary, thinking about your own worth poisons your self-confidence. Not thinking of yourself is the key to your future happiness. Self-esteem seems to be a hot topic today. Schools have special curricula designed to give kids self-esteem. In business they talk about the relationship between self-esteem and job performance. On talk shows you hear people talk about how they have lots of problems because their self-esteem is low. I don't think self-esteem is a problem, unless you make it a problem.

By this statement I represent both the problem and the solution to the problem. So much credence and energy is given to validating one's worth, that the very proposition is self-defeating. It may seem too glib to simply say, "You don't have to prove yourself," but this is in fact true. To whom? is the natural question. As soon as you name whatever audience or person or institution which sits in judgment, you are dependent. The motivational courses that suggest you stand in front of the mirror and praise yourself, or that you use self-affirming mantras to remind yourself of how good you are, miss the essential point that you are who you are anyway. If you never recite another self-affirmation, you are still you. If you denigrate or put yourself down, you are still you. These exercises are not helpful, in my opinion, and they divert you from what could be helpful, and that is building who you want to become.

I believe we can depend on our potential. We may not be satisfied with our lot in life, with our financial, social, or family situation, but we do have the power to change all that. We can learn. We can start any moment to build a better life for ourselves. We can draw inspiration from thousands of heroes and role models, and we can become more than we are. Our only obstacles are our self-doubts, our worries about our essential worth, and our self-pitying rationalizations for giving up. Sometimes I believe we fabricate issues that take away from enjoying ourselves and appreciating the opportunities we have.

I was out of town with a group of people one time, and we started talking about how we slept. One guy mentioned that he had a heck of a time sleeping in a strange bed when on the road, especially with a different pillow than he was used to. Another guy mentioned he slept just fine as long as the bed was super firm. Then one of the guys asked, "I'm curious. When you sleep, do you sleep with your arms outside or inside of the blankets?"

One of the other guys said, "I don't know; what difference does it make?"

"Well, I was just curious if anyone else thought about it," the first man said.

That night the man who was asked the question got no sleep. First he became aware that he usually slept with his arms outside. He thought about calling the guy and telling him the answer to his survey. But then he decided he'd try to sleep with his arms inside the blankets. He just lay there thinking, "It's really warmer than I'd like," so he took his arms out. In a few minutes he was thinking, "This is awful cold." He couldn't believe he usually slept that way. So he put his arms back under the covers. He got no sleep all night.

Fabricating this issue is a lot like discussing self-esteem. It's not a negotiable or deliberate issue. Self-esteem is a state of being ready to act because you value yourself. It's not because you've decided you have earned the chance to succeed; it's because you have always had the choice. You have always had the power to grow, learn, become, achieve, and have the kind of life you want. What many of us lack is a clear idea of what we really want. Chances are, we'd be happy if we could just live our lives acting upon many of the traditional values we've been taught by our parents, teachers, neighbors, and friends all our lives. By the way, most values don't focus on you. Most values at least imply some kind of relationship with others. They define how you act in relation to others, and this is the real key to emotional intelligence.

Even the most simple of encounters between people can create opportunities for growth or can create distress. People who know how to act to keep relationships positive and enjoyable on some level have more emotional intelligence than people who fail to acknowledge others. Some people will define this as having good self-esteem, being able to extend themselves beyond their own issues. I define it as being realistic. Unless you prefer solitary confinement, happiness is best attained through relating positively with other people. If you encounter other people in your life, you need to both give of yourself and receive wisdom from others. This is how positive relationships are built. Negative relationships almost always leave out either the giving or receiving.

Core Values Are Rock-Solid Assets

I believe we acquire values throughout our lives, mainly through relationships we have with people and through the environments in which we live. Core values are perpetual reservoirs of self-wisdom we can share with others. Decisions people make in all areas of their lives should be guided by the same values, but this is not necessarily the case today. Many people view their jobs as separate from their personal lives, and they think and act differently at work than they do at home. I believe the values you use in making decisions in your work life should be identical to the values that may influence you in making decisions in your family and social lives.

To get at your core values takes some time and quiet introspection. Core values are the most important or the most fundamental beliefs you have about who you are and who you want to be. This doesn't mean that core values are complex or esoteric; rather, they are simple and meaningful. We rarely step back and ask ourselves what it is we believe, but doing so is the first step toward gaining self-control.

I happened to be out of town consulting with a client not too long ago, and I lost my wallet. Actually, my wallet is somewhat unconventional, more like a wad of money wrapped around a few credit cards, my license, and a couple pictures with a rubber band. I had walked from my motel to a convenience store, and when I returned, I couldn't find my wallet. I went back to the store, but nobody had found it. After about thirty minutes of retracing my steps, I figured it was a lost cause. After some righteous self-criticism, I went back to my room, and I saw the red light flashing on my phone. My wife had called and left a message.

I called her back, and to my surprise she said, "Did you lose your money?"

I said, "Well yeah, how did you know?"

She said, "A young man just called me and asked for you, and he said he had found your money. He's staying with his grandfather at the Motel 6 in Nisswa."

So I called the number, and a person who sounded like he was nine or ten answered the phone. I said, "My name is Don Wohlenhaus. You found my money?"

And he said "Yup, I got it."

His grandfather told me this story. This young man had found my money in the parking lot, but at first he didn't tell his grandfather. When the boy got back from the store, he went in the bathroom and shut the door. He was in there about fifteen minutes before his grandfather asked if he was okay.

"Yeah, I'm okay," said the boy.

"Well, what are you doing in there?" asked the grandfather.

"Nothing." It was quiet. In a few minutes he came out with a sheepish look on his face, and he said, "Grandpa, look what I found in the parking lot." Of course the sight of all that money was just as shocking for him.

"What are you going to do with it?" asked the grandfather, knowing now that the boy had been wrestling with a moral dilemma in the bathroom. The boy had already decided he was going to return the money. He told his grandfather one of the reasons he decided to return the money was that he saw a laminated picture of my grandson in the wallet. He told his grandfather, "It looks almost like me. He must be a nice man. We should give the money back."

When the boy handed me the wallet, I took a one-hundred-dollar bill from that money and gave it to him. I said, "I hope this is not the first time that you are rewarded for living your values. But I'm glad that it's the first time with me. You are an honorable person." It is very important to let other people know you appreciate their good decisions. Acknowledging them shows respect and humility, and receiving positive feedback reinforces the values upon which the person acted.

One of this little boy's core values was compassion. The Golden Rule, "Do unto others as you would have them do unto you," was what motivated his noble act of honesty. Everyone has values. You can make judgments that these particular values are good, this one is bad, or this one is selfish, and so on, but to the value holder, they make sense. They explain the real world as that person has experienced it. I never discount another's values as unimportant because I know that people act upon their values, regardless of which values they happen to be. Rather than condemn the person for having values I think are self-defeating, I want every person to know he or she has a choice to hold on to those values or to let them go and replace them with values that affirm his or her greatness, precisely because the choice is perpetually available.

Countless situations in business require us to use our values to make decisions. Compassionate decisions can exist beyond an individual, personal level. For instance, the company that extends a sale price even though the buyer was unaware of the sale shows compassion. A business that finds a new job elsewhere in the company for a veteran employee rather than laying him or her off shows the values of loyalty and commitment. Wouldn't everyone prefer to be part of the companies that demonstrate the values we admire? Company values guide all employees and are manifest in how they treat customers, co-workers, vendors, and even competitors.

What you can conclude about individual values, attitudes, and performance is applicable to corporate values, attitudes, and performance. However, companies face greater challenges in accommodating possibly differing values from more people who may participate in the decision making. Business ethics as a course of study in MBA programs, and popular books and speakers who write and talk about principled leadership and socially responsible policies show the importance of which values we apply to business decisions.

I believe attitudes predict behavior, and attitudes are expressions of core values. If people have negative attitudes, based on values such as, "Me first," "Get while the getting is good," or "I deserve to be taken care of," their performance is going to reflect these views and be seen as selfish, distrustful, or dependent. On the other hand, people who believe, "If it's to be, it's up to me," or "I want the opportunity," or "When do I start?" are likely to be seen as eager to learn and easier to teach, and are more likely to be productive.

Perhaps the individual with a negative attitude has really gotten knocked down in life or works out of a poverty-conscious mode, and thus thinks there will never be enough to go around. I can understand that. But whatever the negative experience may have been, the choice of a negative attitude leads to misery. People with negative attitudes give away their power to every person or event that enters their lives. If they are not successful, it's always someone else's fault. Perhaps their bitterness, cynicism, and contempt for mankind are justified. But they're still miserable, and chances are they love company. But I believe even these individuals have choices. Henry Ford once said, "Think you can or think you can't, you're right!"

We Choose Our Assets

Uncertainty and anxiety about the future are a fact of life today in our country in particular. People are finally coming to grips. Government can't give us what we want. We're dismantling our welfare system. Companies can't guarantee us a job. Schools can't seem to guarantee an education that will get you a job anymore. It's up to you. If you are going to be self-reliant, you are going to be marketable. You have to tap into the only thing that you've got, which is your mind. This is why you better have a good understanding of what you want and what's important. With self-understanding you have the capacity for unlimited growth; without it you are likely to be a casualty of inevitable change.

This is an exciting time. It's challenging to us because we might prefer to believe circumstances and other people have more control of our lives than we do. But in a democratic political environment with a capitalistic economic structure functioning well, we truly have free enterprise. This means we have free access to doing business, we can participate fully in investment opportunities, and we have equity in the system. Our very first and most profitable long-term investment should be in our selves. What kind of asset value belongs to You, Inc.?

J. Edgar Hoover said, "Even crooks and gangsters have values. The question is, "Do you share those values?"" Are there certain standards of thought and behavior that are inherently right and that can be accepted as good, or at least as better than their opposites or alternatives? To decide on "better" values takes a high level of emotional intelligence. In my seminars and consulting with individuals and groups, I start with a values inventory. To help articulate what I mean by values, I disclaim umbrella descriptions like "Christian" or "humanistic" or "practical." These are religious or generalized embodiments which many times are used to make a person sound like they have the right values, but really don't tell you what those values are. Generalizing is not productive; individualizing is.

Prioritizing your values is enlightening. We all act on our values, that's a fact. But consciously acting on our values is how we grow and learn and teach others how to act. Sometimes we discover our values when we are acting in a way that makes us feel uncomfortable. When something inside you says, "That's not me," your conscious realization, or conscience, is explaining why you feel awkward. The dissonance helps us all to act literally responsibly. We hold ourselves up to our own standards.

Be self-aware! One of the longest-running best-selling business books is still Richard Bolles' *What Color Is Your Parachute?* which is primarily a self-inventory. The author understands that self-awareness is where you must begin if you are to control your future. We are all products of where we've been and what we've done, but our experiences still don't equal who we are. Decisions are an expression of personal values. When you make a decision, you are letting people know what you stand for. If your values are clear and prioritized and you have formed habits of behavior and decision making around them, future decisions are effortless and can happen very quickly.

My mother used to tell me to always tell a truthful story because then I would never have to remember what I had said when I told the story again. Values are similar guides to your decision making and behavior. If you are true to your values, you know you can defend any decisions you make. There is a difference between espoused values and values in action. In many cases, the espoused values are intellectually appealing. They're logical, apparently positive, and usually deemed socially acceptable and safe. Unfortunately, many of these "no brainer" values are, in practice, difficult to act upon.

On a personal level, perhaps one of your values may be friendship. You make a date to do something with a friend. But on one occasion you are asked to work overtime to finish a project that may mean a great deal of money and recognition in your job. Deciding to abandon your date with your friend can be rationalized in lots of ways, but the bottom line is that your espoused value has limits.

Other values can conflict, compete, and even override the most admirable of values. We all need a sense of why we make the decisions we do. By understanding our decisions, we will arrive at the true hierarchy of the values in the actions we choose. If we are aware of what we really want, we can always choose to act differently.

Please complete the following individual values exercise right now according to the directions on the next two pages.

Values Exercise
Part One

1. Select ten values that are most important to you as guides for how to behave and make decisions in your chosen work.
2. Put a check mark by that value.
3. Then cross out five to bring your list down to just five values.

Achievement	Flexibility
Advancement	Freedom
Challenges	Friendship
Change	Growth
Character	Having a family
Competence	Helping others
Competition	Honesty
Cooperation	Honor
Creativity	Independence
Decency	Inner harmony
Decisiveness	Integrity
Economic security	Intelligence
Effectiveness	Interdependence
Entrepreneurism	Justice
Excellence	Knowledge
Expertise	Leadership
Fame	Loyalty
Financial gain	Maximum effort

Meaningful work	Security
Merit	Self-respect
Money	Self-understanding
Organization	Serenity
Patience	Stability
Personal relationships	Status
Power	Trusting relationships
Predictability	Truth
Privacy	Wealth
Recognition	Wisdom
Reputation	Work
Responsibility	Working relationships

These are suggested values; please add more of your own that you feel are important.

Values Exercise
Part Two

List the five most important personal values to you below:

1. _____

2. _____

3. _____

4. _____

5. _____

Consider the following ideas in regard to each value you have chosen:

1. How does this value apply to a recent decision you've made?

2. What situation would make applying this value more difficult?

3. How would your life be different, especially in your work, if this value was practiced?

4. What would the business organization be like if it encouraged employees to practice this value?

I encourage everybody I know to make an inventory of their own values. The idea is to enable individuals to examine or reexamine their value systems and come to greater self-awareness. I hope you've done that now.

Just like an individual, the company needs to prioritize positive values it sees as essential. What the company does is more important than what it says, which is also true for the individual, and the conscious exercise of defining its values will help shape its future behavior. Communicating with others and acting through various roles and relationships challenge everybody to work together and avoid potentially negative conflicts. It's critical that companies become more self-aware, reinforcing values that will help set expectations, provide aspirations, and encourage the best performance from everyone. Don't discount this part of your business. It's vital.

Business Equity

➤ **Productivity improves** because the people doing the work improve their performance.

➤ **Managers need to develop their leadership skills** to support employees and to hold them accountable for their own performance.

➤ **Caring for employees (rather than caretaking)** and caring about the customer are hallmarks of leadership that derive from the core values of a company. Companies who care for people have tremendous equity.

Chapter Three
Business Equity

CORPORATE VALUES are more important than developing eloquent mission statements and making signs that say, "We love our customers!" One area in which the company shows its values is in the way it relates to its work force. By eliminating job hazards, for instance, a company demonstrates it respects its employees. By offering employee stock ownership opportunities, a company demonstrates the value of inclusion and teamwork. Clarifying values can either precede the adoption of new policies or may help to communicate why some policies exist in the first place.

The policies most important to the issue of corporate values are the ones that are practiced on a daily basis. How the organization relates to its own members, its customers, the community in which it operates, and the rest of the world of business becomes its institutional equity. We're accustomed to quantifying equity in terms of dollar value and share of ownership, but I maintain there is more to the life of a business than descriptive statistics. Its equity is its reputation. The visitor, the new employee, the new customer all experience a company's equity in their first impression. The disappointing experience belies a low equity, and further depletes the company's equity treasury. On the other hand, a positive experience both advertises the company's wealth and adds to it.

Many companies understand that their long-term prosperity is grounded in doing the right things in the short term. How they do business on a daily basis translates to long-term reputation. Who wouldn't rather work for a company everyone admires? Good companies have less trouble recruiting. Who wouldn't benefit from being associated in some way with the best in the business? When customers, vendors, and suppliers want to work with you, you don't have to worry so much about the competition. The return on investments in equity are long-lasting, but they're based in how the company operates every day.

I teach a four-week course on values for businesses in the Upper Midwest. In the beginning we spend four hours on what I call a values workshop. We discuss forty values that I think apply to all successful businesses.

Then I say, "We want to make this concept of values practical and meaningful for this business, so in the next hour and a half, let's get these forty down to ten." The participants discuss relative values, eliminate duplicates, and everyone gets to vote on which values they believe the company should stand for. How do you feel about integrity? How do you feel about honesty?—or trustworthiness? How do these show up in our business dealings?

And those ten will be put on the board. Now I ask them to get those down to five. "What we want to do is keep our ultimate mission (based upon these five values) fairly simple; let's see if we can all agree on five." My rationale is that better decisions are made by a company that knows its core or most basic values and that everyone must buy into these values. We spend another hour going through the ten to get to five.

A great deal of cynicism and nay-saying takes place among some managers when we focus on values. Misunderstanding and resistance to change are two of the main reasons. The misunderstanding occurs when values aren't seen as being important or aren't considered bottom-line enough. Either idea is shortsighted and naïve. Most management advice of the past century has focused on measuring outputs. We judge productivity on the basis of investment and return, on profits, but we have lost sight of what generates our profits. People do. And the quality of work that people do is not automatic, cannot be commanded, and shouldn't be taken for granted.

The Pines at Grand View Lodge

The Pines at Grand View Lodge is a golf resort located in northern Minnesota. Their customers have consistently given them a ninety percent or better rating for lodging, food, golf, and service. Better than sixty percent of their business is from repeat customers. In 1995, it was rated as one of the top golf resorts in the United States by *Golf Digest*. When I first started working with Grand View, we gathered all the year-round employees in the off-season and met for eight hours to determine what Grand View's values would be. We followed the procedure outlined above.

Bringing the ten values down to five took about two hours. The discussion was lively and meaningful. It was obvious to me that these people had a clear understanding of the importance of values and that they wanted to make sure the selected five values represented what they felt should be most important at Grand View in making all decisions regarding the business. (Their dedication was such that they could not reduce the ten to five. So they decided to go with six values—why not?)

The following explanation is intended to show how this one company translated the abstract to the concrete. They didn't see this as an intellectual exercise. They were quite serious about committing themselves and each other to these values in action.

- Responsibility
- Integrity
- Cooperation
- Excellence
- Personal Development
- Loyalty

The leadership at Grand View encouraged them to explain how they felt the values should apply in their work.

Responsibility: Individuals should be responsible for their work performance first to themselves, next to their co-workers, and then to the organization.

Integrity: Integrity involves having intimate working relationships with everyone in the organization. Intimate means open and honest communication with each other, including with leadership.

Cooperation: Teamwork is cooperation. Each individual understands that cooperation is a primary expectation of everyone at Grand View, especially leadership. Example: When a major wind storm hit the resort in 1995 and blew down over a hundred trees, and tree branches were scattered all over the resort, everyone, including leadership, pitched in and the cleanup was accomplished in two days.

Another example comes to mind. When the season was coming to a close in October of 1995, most of the seasonal staff had left. A major company booked a three-day stay. All year-round people, including leadership, waited tables and provided guest services without a hitch. Most companies would like their people to work together as a team, but to make this happen in crises, the organization has to have already selected cooperation as a value and has had to have already practiced cooperation daily.

Excellence: The people at Grand View decided excellence meant providing lodging, food, golf, and service experiences second to none in their business category. They want word of mouth to be their most effective form of advertising. They want to feel the pride in knowing the work they do is meaningful and appreciated. Their measure of customer satisfaction is when the customer's expectations have been exceeded. Examples: Rooms are exceptionally clean and comfortable. Walleye dinners are cooked to perfection and are served to guests by someone who knows them by name. Golfers are met by young men and women who unload their golf clubs, clean them and place them in their carts. Customers are not surprised to find the tee times they had made six months before when they booked their rooms are just as they had arranged: 8:20 A.M.

Personal Development: Personal development programs are provided for all staff people year-round. The focus of these programs is emotional intelligence. Leaders at Grand View hire intelligent individuals for seasonal work, mostly college students. These men and women want to learn how to become more employable when they complete their schooling, and Grand View gives them this opportunity. All staff people want the opportunity to grow and prosper personally right along with the company.

Loyalty: Leaders at Grand View believe that an employee's first loyalty should be to co-workers, not to the organization. If you are loyal to your co-workers, company loyalty will follow.

When anyone is hired at Grand View, these six values are presented to them, in writing. Individuals are asked to look at their personal values and see how they match up with Grand View's. If they do fit well, intimate relationships are more likely to develop. All decisions at Grand View flow from these values. This is why everyone there makes good decisions quickly.

Productivity and Core Values

When I first make a presentation to a new client prospect, I'm used to some skepticism and some resistance to my ideas on the part of the prospect. Talking about emotional intelligence and feelings and values seems to make some people uncomfortable. The following conversation is really a composite of many discussions I've had with prospects.

"But Don, we don't have the time for a lot of hand-holding and classes about how people feel. And, frankly, I'm more concerned with them getting the job done right, on time, and under budget than I am about how they feel about their work. I'm paying for their productivity."

"Are you getting as much productivity as you want? I understood you to say there may be a problem here. Would you be in favor of doing whatever is necessary if it increases productivity?"

"Yes, of course. As a manager, that's what I must be accountable for."

Those who care about the bottom line must eventually acknowledge that productivity is what generates profits, and productivity is influenced more by core values than by talking about what profits should be. An obsessive fixation on short-term profits and an unwillingness to acknowledge work motivations other than money stifle investment and reduce productivity.

"Do you think you are different from your employees? I mean do you think what motivates you is different from what motivates them?"

"No. But I think sometimes I take my role more seriously, and I push myself harder than my employees do."

"Why is that, do you think?"

"Well, I have more responsibility. It's because that's what I'm expected to do."

"In other words, if your employees felt the same self-motivation you feel, they'd be more apt to push themselves like you do, is this a fair assumption?"

"Yes. But to tell the truth, at seven-fifty per hour, I don't expect them to do more than the minimum."

"Well, this is distressing to hear," I said, "because I think you're wasting your money, and you may be blaming your employees for what may be your problem."

Assuming low-paid workers can't, won't, or shouldn't produce great work because they don't make much money is a big mistake. Some business owners expect so little of their employees, that they've given up trying to relate positively to them. Expecting very little, or worse, expecting poor performance kills any possibility for a healthy, positive working relationship. How some managers view their employees is at the root of the company's productivity problem. This is typical of what I hear:

"I feel a certain anger when I sense my employees don't care as much as I do about the company. Some of them are just plain lazy, and they are a real pain to deal with."

"You have certain expectations, I understand. What happens when employees fall short? What do you do?"

Leadership Comes from Core Values

When I sense a manager is talking about an issue of leadership rather than performance, I discuss this with them so that they understand the difference. If you're a manager and you haven't shifted your focus to leadership, then negative employee attitudes, poor morale, and low performance are solely your responsibility. Caretaking management indicates that you have a low level of emotional intelligence, and it encourages unacceptable behavior and performance. Stop caretaking people.

You have to change from the idea of managing people to leading people. Being an effective leader today requires you take responsibility for growing people, not managing them. You influence their behavior by what you do to help them, not by what you tell them to do. If you do not require them to be responsible and accountable by following through with firm penalties for poor performance, you will lose their respect.

If you move them to another department, you're care-taking them, and you will also lose their respect. You'll also lose the respect of the new manager. You will have lost the opportunity for you to develop your leadership potential.

If you decide to let the difficult people remain within the organization, you must care for them rather than care-take them. You must:

1. Explain what the values of the organization are.
2. Encourage them to develop their personal values in writing.
3. Ask them to compare their values with those of the organization. Explain that if their values don't match up well with the values of the organization, the relationship will not work.
4. Put in writing the five primary expectations you have of them. Inspect these expectations weekly. People respect what you inspect, not what you say you expect.
5. Define what the penalties are if the employee fails to meet the company's expectations.
6. Enforce the penalties.

The leader deals with difficult people with humility, compassion, and firmness. You listen to the employee in order to understand their motivations, not to sympathize with or analyze their reasoning. You challenge them to grow in their emotional intelligence, to choose to develop their potential. You set a good example of what that looks like—that's leadership. I've yet to meet an employee who wanted to fail, but I've met hundreds who did not know how to be peak performers.

Challenging people to grow forces you to grow. Many managers are uncomfortable with the change from managing to leading because they were always taught to be managers, not leaders. In my work with managers we first determine if you want to be a leader. Here are some benefits:

1. You can eliminate distress from your work.
2. Your people will have positive feelings.
3. You'll see that peak performance follows positive feelings.
4. You'll experience shorter and more effective meetings.
5. You'll have more time for learning.
6. You'll have more optimism.
7. You'll be more creative.
8. Your people will turn complaints into solutions.

Your success as a leader requires that you have a clear understanding of your own values and of the values that your company practices. Building your own asset value and being able to contribute to the company's equity at the same time are not pie-in-the-sky ideals. Self-development and corporate equity building go on daily in productive companies.

Cheryl Johnson's Leadership

I met Cheryl Johnson in 1984. She was sales manager at the Radisson Hotel in St. Paul. I called on her to sell her advertising on the radio, and we hit it off. There are just some people with whom you seem to be on the same wavelength. Common values and a certain maturity account for it.

She has tremendous self-confidence. She listens for feeling, and not just for content. In our meeting I made some attempts to sell her an advertising contract. She listened to me but kept asking open-ended questions about me and about radio, "Does it really work? How does it work? Why should I use it?"

To answer her questions I had to start asking her questions such as, "What is the turnover rate here?"

She said that normally her industry had very high employee turnover rate, but that was not the case at the Radisson St. Paul. "Because I don't let it happen," she began. "Because I like to develop people, and the only way I know of to do that is to make a commitment and put their interest up front and work with them." I was trying to sell her advertising, and she was teaching me why her employees were loyal. She knew her business, and now I know it better, too. Listening to her, I was able to custom design a more successful advertising program for her. She has a great track record of helping people focus on what's important.

She has an extraordinary ability to get people to be self-motivated because she believes in their ability to do a good job. Selling for a hotel, selling rooms or selling group functions, is very demanding work. Price is always an issue. Oftentimes it gets to be the only issue for the customer, but Cher deals with these situations constructively. One day a salesperson came in and announced, "Well, I can't sell this package because the competition is selling it for less."

She sat down with him and replied, "Right, they are selling it for less, but look at what they've got and let's look at what we've got. The indoor pool. The nicer rooms. The better service. The better food. Better location. Free parking. Can we focus on that? Let's do that before we get into cutting our price."

She gets her people to look at value first and then consider the price. This is not only the way she personally buys, but she has transferred her standards and values to help the company compete in the marketplace. The idea that price has no meaning without considering value is both a personal and business truism which fast-buck salespeople and price-bound customers don't understand. She tries to teach this particular value to both her employees and the customer.

She also is the kind of person who understands that the whole hotel staff has to work together. For example, one of her salespeople came in and said, "The food service screwed up my sales, and I'm not going to stand losing this sale. Food service sent the wrong cheese tray to the executive who was staying here and messed it all up. I'm not going to put up with this anymore. Enough is enough!"

Cher said, "Well, why don't we talk with the people in food service? Why don't we try to communicate with them?"

"Well, what am I supposed to do? I've already told them that they screwed up."

Cher said, "That's not what I'm saying. What we want to do is try and get them to come up here and spend maybe an hour or two with us when we're communicating with someone who is going to stay here and let them listen to what the requests or needs are." So she brought the salesperson in with the food service manager to meet with the customer.

The customer said, "Now listen, I'm not the key person; the key person is the president of the company. He's the one that's going to be staying in that room up there, and he's a very demanding guy, and you could make my life a lot easier. He likes Diet Coca-Cola in his room. He likes Perrier water. He likes pure ice. I don't know if you've got a pure-ice company here. Like North Star. He wants that. He doesn't want ice out of the machine. So put a bag of the real pure ice and let him see the bag. And he likes a cheese tray or something. Don't give him a normal cheese tray. Give him something that is really classy because he's going to have people coming into the room and that cheese tray is a reflection on who he is. Not who you are, but who he is. Can you do that?"

The food service person heard all this, and when the customer left, Cher turned to him and said, "You see, we in marketing are not making these demands, our customers are." The conflict resolution here is not who is more right or wrong, the salesperson or the food service department, but who can meet the customer's standards, who exceeds the customer's expectations. Subsequent to this event, by the way, food service and marketing put together some Polaroid pictures of cheese trays that people had thought were really outstanding. Now once the customer selects a picture of what kind of tray they have in mind, food service uses it as a guideline.

Cher deals with business decisions based on the shared company value of customer satisfaction. No chastisement. No anger. Get everybody together, explain the situation, and actually create an example of what might be done. Besides happier, more satisfied customers, of course, her management style develops her employees' problem-solving and communication skills, which partially accounts for her property's very low employee turnover rate.

People like Cher make decisions based on their value systems. What she did was to go back to what was right with the customer and organize and engineer her people to serve the customer. The value that she's working from is not, "Do this because I told you to; that's what we get paid for."

She said, "Look, are we serving the customer? If we are, then everybody is going to be fine."

Work Evolution

➤ **The demise of the job description** is an indication of what really matters on the job—the work that needs to be done.

➤ **Activity as a way to measure productivity is out;** positive attitudes and work ethics influence the quality of work performed. These are the new measures of productivity.

Chapter Four

Work Evolution

J OHN IS DOING WORK he does not like merely for a paycheck. That is not enough.

Wendy is balking at change; her company wants her to accept new responsibilities in areas for which she has not been trained.

Barbara can't afford to give up health care benefits, can't take time off from work to attend school, and feels trapped in a dead-end job.

Bill just graduated from college and is frustrated that the job market appears mythical. People don't appreciate his degree as much as he thought they would.

Many people are disappointed in their careers. They don't like their jobs. I believe these people have lost sight of their values. They don't know what's important for themselves, and they also don't know what's important for their potential employer.

Many people want their jobs more than they care about themselves. They put tremendous stock in the position, the title, or the office they inhabit. All this investment in the ideal position is ultimately no guarantee of anything. Unfortunately, in the current culture, jobs are disappearing. What is left is work.

The "Peter Principle," from a book by the same title, asserts that people rise to the highest level of their incompetence. Through typical career moves, they steadily get promoted to positions with responsibilities for which they have little expertise. The great sales achiever, for instance, may be rewarded by being advanced to a sales management position. The skill sets for success in sales can be very different than for management, and the idea that the former salesperson will continue to succeed is not based on any particular evidence. If the salesperson does succeed at his or her first management position, chances are more promotions with increasing management responsibilities will probably result. If he or she is a terrible manager, promotion probably won't happen. Two tragedies result. The company loses a great salesperson's productivity, and salespeople get stuck with a poor manager.

Companies today are looking for evidence of competence and are demanding more accountability than ever. One of the positive results of competition and corporate cost cutting is a greater emphasis on accountability and productivity. Promotions given out to reward performance only make sense if the individual promoted can do the new job well. Promotions are not merely granted by virtue of how long a particular worker has had the job, as they once were. With downsizing and layoffs in the thousands hitting all levels of management, workers must demonstrate more productivity just to keep the jobs they already have.

What many careerists are learning is that they need to evolve in their own career path. They need to grow and learn new skills in order to move up. They must be able to adapt, be flexible, and most of all produce in new and changing environments. The rewards will go to those people who are able to acquire new skills and who are able to adapt quickly. Our greatest assets are not our past successes but our present abilities to be successful with new challenges to our competence. A person's success in life has more to do with what he or she tries than how good they are at first. It's the investment in learning that pays off. Someone who really wants to move up in a company should be looking for things that are not going well for the company. Fixing that problem could be a way to get a promotion.

No Job Descriptions

Welcome to the new world of work, a world filled with opportunities but subject to new rules and game plans that are, if nothing else, flexible. When I first heard of downsizing, early retirements, and restructuring, I believed that these changes were occurring primarily in manufacturing and large corporations. The reality is that all businesses, institutions, organizations, and governing bodies are changing due to both global pressures (competition, new technology) and internal pressures (efficiency and expediency). What is also interesting is that many companies are not merely cutting their work forces to save costs. They're outsourcing work their own employees used to do, and they're recruiting new employees who have skills they need rather than trying to retrain present employees.

For many people caught in corporate upheaval or career changes, the permanent job isn't there anymore. Layoffs, downsizing, reengineering, reorganizing, flattening, all of these changes seem to threaten the very idea of having a career in managing other people. Actually the picture isn't bleak; it's full of new opportunities. What is changing is the way managers and employees both need to do their jobs in order to contribute to the productivity of the company. There is no room, time, or budget for managers or employees who do not increase productivity. How to do that is what this book is all about.

Equating what the job description says with who you are if you accept that description is a chief cause of anxiety and grief for many people. Unfortunately many working people find themselves chugging along on what's called a "job-identity" track. Some people define themselves and others by the trappings of job status, and almost obsessively demand to know your level of job attainment.

"I'm with IBM; I'm the executive director for a major non-profit; I'm the manager for the West Coast Sales and Marketing division; I work in the district office; I'm with Cargill, corporate." Well, if you identify with the job and believe this is really who you are, what happens when the job disappears? Unfortunately, a lot of laid-off managers spent many years deciding they were managers for such and such company, and now they don't have a clue about who they are.

Job security in the U.S. has been blasted right into space. Thousands of managers who identified with positions are now discovering that they were misled, or that they have bought a bogus ticket. They learn that the job is not who they are, but they're lost for a way to identify themselves. This is what has made the out-placement industry one of the fastest growing industries in the economy. Psychologists, support groups, and a plethora of self-help books, tapes, and seminars have become very popular. Now they're saying, "Who am I? If I'm not the district director for this company in St. Paul, Minnesota, because my job's just been eliminated, who am I?"

The unemployed manager goes out for a job interview and feels lost, and is lost, and has no self-confidence or self-esteem. Perhaps this laid-off manager might have stopped growing ten years before because the company owned him or her. Perhaps he or she settled into a comfort zone.

The higher up the ladder you went, the less work you had to do. What does it mean when chief executives and upper-level management make a hundred times more money than frontline employees? Too much of the time management perks have been more visible than management accountability. With layers of management and big staffs many of the large companies encouraged the "get your work done through others" philosophy. According to this management advice, the successful manager should personally do the least work while manipulating the most work out of subordinates. As the ranks of people successful at getting others to do work has swelled, the processes for decision making and productivity itself have suffered. Management hasn't been alone in costing companies lots of money for perks that do not influence productivity.

But now, in the face of competition and under the guise of efficiency, many people, both managers and their nonexempt underlings, are being fired. Managers are being told, "We don't need you anymore; get back in the marketplace."

Some managers I know today are going from eighty-five thousand to one hundred thousand dollars a year down to a job that pays twenty-five thousand dollars, and this job requires the person to actually work fourteen hours a day to earn it. It's easy to understand the emotional cries, "I'm lost. I can't believe this. You people have let me down."

Activity Means Less and Less

The real employment problem America faces is not with companies downsizing. Nor is it with bloated management positions. The problem is not due to too many benefits for employees. The problem is with how we have viewed our jobs in this country. On both the management and employee levels, the proposition has been the same: the job is what most companies provide. The work to be done has been delegated from the top down, and everyone has had a job title or place on an organizational chart which is supposed to define their duties, their contribution to the company's product or service. But this organizational structure doesn't work anymore.

Manual labor is easy to quantify, piecework can be measured, hours can be tallied, and relative market forces can determine pay scales and compensation. But these measures are all appropriate for reproducing work. They account for quantity of time or effort put in, but do not describe intangibles like quality, creativity, or other contributions toward productivity that are increasingly more important in this global economy. Both automation and higher technology have replaced millions of jobs people previously did, and this trend will certainly continue.

In the past a job was very well prescribed, meaning the duties, responsibilities, and so forth were spelled out. I was once given a job description in sales which specified that I should cover a particular territory, with specific accounts to call on, with specific expectations for what business I was to generate from those accounts. The sales manager typically didn't like too much deviation from this grand plan, and all the measurements of my success were activity driven. A specific number of cartons and cases needed to be sold to each client, their inventory needed my monitoring, and I needed to fill their quota of purchases each month or there would be serious repercussions. There really wasn't any need or encouragement for the salesperson to exercise creativity and imagination.

People still cling to the idea that if the salesperson makes "x" number of calls, a certain percentage will close, and the trick is just in keeping the number "x" high. Quantity of activity is supposed to determine productivity. This can be disastrous. Recently, the president of one of my client companies put out a mandate requiring an 11.5-percent increase in sales for 1995. The people that run the key division in the company knew that the trend was around four percent, and the president's expectation caused them great concern. Over the next two months I observed this division putting all their efforts into data gathering in order to substantiate to the president of the company why the four-percent increase was more realistic. The morale of the people in that division fell to new lows. All they were doing was gathering data to substantiate what they already knew to someone who didn't want to believe it anyway.

I have to admit that when I was a salesman, I would lie on those activity reports all the time. When I was hired, I was told I had to make thirty calls a day. Sitting around at lunch with about twenty salespeople, we'd create our reports. We actually did about ten sales calls a day. But I'd suggest twenty-one, and Bill would put down twenty, and someone else would put down twenty-two, and we'd all trade off being the top guy from day to day. Eventually I was promoted into management myself, charged with reading those reports. I've always doubted the relevance of this system, and not just because the numbers are usually cooked! There's just no respect for individuality, personal or professional growth, or for building customer relationships. There are no expectations for learning anything. Energy is wasted by forcing activity and presuming that the numbers will lead to more business.

Attitude Means More and More

Attitude is more important than activity. Today my best advice for hiring salespeople is different. I do not care if the candidate has any experience at all in selling the product. Today I can give him a ninety-minute video showing him the features and benefits of what we're selling from which he can learn techniques and skills about selling. But what I can't do is give him a ninety-minute video on accountability and responsibility and trustworthiness. The very best I can do is sense that he or she has these qualities. If I at least can recognize and build on those, the sales will follow. I look for positive work ethics, and I want the candidate to demonstrate that he or she knows what they are. I will ask candidates to give me an example of their application of work ethics in their work histories.

Whether you're preparing for a new job or are in the midst of re-defining your role in your present job, and whether or not you are now in a management position, you'll have to learn to be more self-reliant in the years ahead. The company, managers, and supervisors used to tell you what to do; now you must take full responsibility for what you do. You might as well throw away your job description. It probably has no relevance at all to the work that has to be done within the organization. What is more important is your willingness to do whatever you need to do to be a contributor.

The demise of the job description is symbolic of a shift in how people relate to each other on the job. Managers in the productivity age will be more effective if they can shift their mindset from seeking and attempting to maintain authoritarian, directive, impersonal control to cultivating a more decentralized, autonomous, empowering style of leadership. They should help motivate and support people instead of monitoring activity. Putting one's faith in following a job description which attempts to describe all the areas for which a person is responsible is not practical or effective in dealing with people. Because companies today are fighting innumerable competitors and are trying to please demanding customers, they want the people who know how to please the client to be making their own decisions about what should be done. Client satisfaction leads to more business. Employee activity is not the measure of productivity.

The client is called many different names, depending upon the industry; for instance, the student and parents are clients of the school system, citizens or the public are the clients of government agencies, and the buyers of goods are the clients of our manufacturing and retail industries. Clients of the service industries demand that workers perform; with most transactions the customer rarely sees a manager. It's the frontline employee's performance that determines how satisfied that client will be.

If a client has a problem, he or she wants it solved regardless of whether or not the solution is part of anybody's job description. Companies today want people who will do what needs doing, as if they owned the company. Go ahead and do it; don't limit yourself. Don't say, "That's not my job."

Now that takes self-reliance. It takes self-responsibility and accountability. It takes confidence. Only employees with a high level of self-esteem can be so invested in their work that they do more than the minimum and constantly exceed the requirements of the job. Some insecure employees think, "What if I make a mistake; what if I do it wrong? The consequences could be very bad for me; I'll be criticized because it isn't part of my job description; I'd better not make a decision on this."

A good leader encourages people to become self-reliant. The company should assist people to pursue a growth path, to seek a high learning curve without limitations inherent in a job description.

I know that what I want out of an employee is more than clock hours. Even if you've only hired the plumber to come out and fix a drain, you sure expect more than the minimum, and what you want, you don't necessarily pay for. You want the plumber to take off his or her shoes. You want them to clean up after themselves. And you may even want a problem solved you weren't even aware needed solving, such as another leak you might not have noticed. We want a professional job done. By professional, we mean done well, with pride. There are professionals in every job category. They distinguish themselves by their attitude, work ethics, and skill level.

Steve Werner's Story

Steve Werner was one of my prize pupils at Grand View Lodge. Steve was one of the people who came over from England in April of 1995 to work as a waiter for the summer. He came to the first seminar, and after the seminar he came up to me and said, "Can I talk to you privately one on one? I really like what you're saying about self-understanding and accountability and personal growth."

We met, and this is what he said: "I go to Oxford in England, but I've never heard any of the stuff you're talking about there. I have received a lot of head knowledge in history and English and math, but what you're talking about, personal growth, personal development, how you go about making choices, decisions, deciding on your values, we're not learning that. I'm really into this and I want to learn this."

And I said, "Fine."

So over the summer I saw him at least once a week. Plus he also attended all four of the seminars scheduled for the staff. I watched Steve's progress in his work. He was doing waiter things better than anybody. For instance, he established immediate rapport with every customer in the restaurant, and they got to know him on a first-name basis. He took more tables than the average waiter. The average waiter, I'd say, might take three or four tables; Steve does six and he does six well. Steve said to me one day, "You know, I see things around the resort that should be done; should I do them?"

I said, "Yes. Like what?"

"We were down at the beach this morning, and the wind had blown up a lot of weeds, obviously not very attractive, and nobody is cleaning it up."

I said, "Well, go ahead, do it." So he did it on his time. He got a pitchfork, went down there with a wheelbarrow, and cleaned up the weeds. This did not go unnoticed by the people he's working with. One of the managers of the resort saw him also. Now Steve's viewed in a different category from all other waiters. Steve has now been elevated in the minds of people as a doer. He's viewed as someone who will see work that needs to be done, and he doesn't wait for someone else to do it; he does it himself.

The resort decided to open another restaurant, with an Italian theme, for the months of July and August. Of course, they looked at their present employees to staff the new venture. They started talking to various people. Steve came to me and said, "What do you think? I'd like to run it."

I said, "Do you feel comfortable doing that? If so, do it." So he stepped up and they gave him the job. He went from waiting tables to cleaning the beach to running the Italian restaurant. Now he's in charge of the staff, in charge of getting the food out and the reservations, the whole operation. He does an extraordinarily good job. This does not go unnoticed by other people working there. It is obvious that he's head and shoulders above most other waiters. Other employees have started to come to Steve saying, "How did you do that?"

I've heard Steve tell them in group meetings, "All you have to do is get your mind into this thing. Make up your mind that you're going to live with your potential. It doesn't matter what your job or job description is supposed to be. You own your work; do the best you know how to do."

This kind of attitude focuses on growth, learning, and increasing competencies, no matter the limited expectations the job may have. Every job is an opportunity to learn more about what you can and can't do, and what you need to learn to improve. Steve says, "Because that's why I'm here. I'm not here for summer vacation. I'm here to learn some real things about life that will help me when I finish college and go into the real world of work—like always do your best, and people will think the best of you." From this perspective, the job as a waiter at Grand View Lodge now looks like a heck of an opportunity.

The best job security is to be the best at what you do, and some companies recognize this is a particular value essential in new hires. Good character traits and positive attitudes are terrific assets to show if you're in the job market or if you wish to be promoted. Most managers and business owners know your growth curve or learning curve is potentially faster and higher than candidates who do not show positive attitudes.

Tom Shannon's Story

Tom Shannon, twenty-four years old, is a fairly typical career seeker who has learned to improvise. In college he had changed his major a couple of times from business to communications and didn't have a real firm sense of what he wanted to do for work. He did some flying while he was in college, and what he really wanted to do was to be a pilot. After college he went to flight school, learned to be a pilot, and went to work for an air charter service. Unfortunately, it didn't last too long; the charter service folded, but he did log about six hundred hours of flying. He tried to get a job at an airline, but for the two positions open, over seven thousand people applied!

After wandering a bit, he found himself working for a radio station in St. Cloud selling radio ads. He called on Dan Huschke, the president of Python's Recycling Company in St. Cloud, a small city in central Minnesota. Dan talked to me the next day about hiring him. He told me he had been very impressed with how Tom Shannon handled himself, how he was a good salesperson, and how he just seemed to have a great attitude. I encouraged Dan to check him out some more, which he did. Dan decided he wanted to recruit him, and he gave him an irresistible offer.

Dan said, "I'd like to hire you. We're a recycling company, as you know, and you will have to start at the bottom. This means unloading trucks, unloading railroad cars, sorting aluminum cans, bottles, paper, cardboard. It's dirty, hard work. If you can handle that well, we don't have a marketing person in our company, so maybe you can work into that. Maybe. I'm not saying for sure. Plus, we do some flying. I happen to be a pilot, and we have reason to fly around to our other recycling centers. Maybe we can work that in to it."

Tom took the job and in two months worked to the point where half the day he spent marketing. Because of his positive attitude and with the prospect of getting to fly, he was on a high learning curve. He started marketing programs and publicity campaigns in St. Cloud to make the company more visible. Leads started pouring in for both suppliers and buyers. He began to explore, research, and write down descriptions of what other companies were doing.

This high-growth mode was not the result of landing his dream job. But at only twenty-four years old, where do you think he'll be at thirty? He will always be very effective in whatever he chooses to do.

Lisa Who Used to Be a Waitress

Hiring people based almost solely upon their character traits is a departure from the norm in most companies today, but that was the basis upon which twenty-two-year-old Lisa Lund also was hired for a job at Python's. Lisa was raised on a farm near Brandon, Minnesota. She had a typical Minnesota farm upbringing, and she expressed solid midwestern values in the hiring interview. I sat in on the preemployment interview with the company department heads. It was obvious to me she could handle herself well anywhere.

Knowing she has turned out to be a terrific employee, I look back at her first interview for some clues that could lead to duplicating this hiring success. How did she develop such confidence at such a young age? How did the company recognize her positive character traits in the interview process?

One of the first jobs Lisa took after high school was as a cocktail waitress; she shared the story with me. She said, "You know, I come from a small town, and since I was twenty-one, I've been working as a cocktail waitress in a big city. St. Cloud has sure been a different experience for me."

"How has it been different?"

"Well," she said, "the money is good, and I've learned a lot about people. I've learned a lot about how to deal with people, particularly people that don't think well of themselves."

I said, "Lisa, why do you want the warehouse position?"

And she said, "I'd like a change right now. Quite frankly I've looked at this position, there's a wide variety of things that can be done in this job, specifically the computer thing, how you're trying to get some software developed for inventory and things like that, and I think I'd like the relationship with the warehouse people." She said, "I think I would enjoy this opportunity right now."

"Well," another interviewer said, "you know you'll be working in a warehouse setting. And the guys in the warehouse have a tendency to speak a language sometimes that's not too pleasant to hear. In fact they get kind of crusty. Will that bother you?"

She looked him right in the eye and she said, "After eighteen months as a cocktail waitress, do you think I would hear anything in the warehouse that I have not heard as a cocktail waitress?"

I said, "Good point."

She continued, "No. Does it bother me? No. Only in the sense that I think it would be nice if they knew how hurtful it is to them rather than to me. It hurts them more than me. If they make a remark about me in a context that is not too nice, I feel badly for them. It's too bad they're not mature enough to understand that's no way to build a working relationship."

I found Lisa to be remarkable for her self-confidence and self-reliance. It is amazing how little age really has to do with maturity. Here she is at the age of twenty-two, and she's already figured out that who she is, is not the same as what her job is. She's figured out a lesson some unemployed managers struggle with to the point of suicide: you're not the job.

She's twenty-two years old. Lisa who was a cocktail waitress is now going to be a warehouse person. Lisa does not identify with the position that she's in. If she's a waitress, she reasons, "That's okay, but that's not who I am." If she is a warehouse person, "That's okay, but that's not who I am. I'm still Lisa who happens to be doing warehouse work." She knows who she is. She also demonstrated in this brief interview a great capacity for compassion. She demonstrated she was eager to learn and that she recognized this as an opportunity for her to grow.

The abilities to think creatively, to rely upon one's own values in dealing with people, to make quick decisions, and to sustain good relationships can be fostered in companies, but some people already have an abundant supply of these abilities and only need the company to encourage their further development. Lisa is one of those people who can improvise and respond appropriately even in unfamiliar territories. I suspect there are millions of Lisas out there, but most companies aren't looking for them. More tragic, perhaps, is that they discourage the development of people like her by assuming "low-level" employees are worth only what they're paid.

But the job and its pay scale have almost nothing to do with the kind of work ethics and potential productivity of most people. People who are self-confident and self-reliant may not have the sophistication of those who have all the answers, but they do understand themselves. Companies that truly want to build the asset value of their work force will seek out, hire, and encourage people like Lisa who have a great work ethic. Encouragement starts with expecting new hires to solve some problems for you. You need to tell people this is what is expected of them, because people aren't used to having this opportunity or responsibility.

New Python's employees and even many veteran employees don't fit into typical two-page job descriptions. They write their own job descriptions, using their initiative, creativity, and positive attitude to decide how they can best contribute to the company. Lisa was hired as the "warehouse administrator," a position which did not exist. But the warehouse manager had said, "We're spending too much time doing paperwork and too much time on the telephone. We need some help!" So they hired her to help.

"Well," she said, "what do I do here?"

Stu Hamilton, the owner, replied, "The very best you can." He went on, "Because Lisa, we expect you to go in there, listen to Kenny and Lloyd and find out what their needs are, and then you will help them with those needs. We want you to solve some problems."

Her face brightened; already she appeared more confident and eager. Stuart explained his understanding of some of her responsibilities, "Probably there'll be invoicing, keeping track of the invoices. Shipping, forms that have to be filled out. You'll have to work with the companies to ship them materials. You'll work with individuals who deliver material to the warehouse so we know what was supposed to be on the truck really was on the truck. You might have to do some scheduling with Kenny and Lloyd, keep track of who's supposed to be where at a certain time because you know something's coming in. But you'll kind of create that position yourself. Do what's needed. How's that sound?"

"Great!" she said.

You bring to any job your talent, skill, experience, and values. A wise employer respects and uses your work ethic. Stu's trust in Lisa's decision-making abilities has already paid off. Not only has Lisa streamlined the office procedures, but she recently saved the company another ton of money—literally. In the warehouse, pallets are used to move around all kinds of material, from aluminum to cardboard to plastics. One of Python's oldest client-suppliers made an urgent call to the president, Dan Huschke. His records showed the same amount had been credited as more valuable only a few days before! Dan took the customer's complaint to Lisa.

"Do we pay the customer for the pallet?" she asked.

"No, of course not," said Dan.

"Well, not anymore!" said Lisa. Apparently Lisa discovered that every load from every supplier was being weighed and credited without subtracting the weight of the pallet, containers, or whatever packaging held the loads together. She knew this wasn't right, and on her own, subtracted out the containers, assuming that was the way it was supposed to be done.

Her decision came from her sense of values—fairness not only to the customer but to the company. Her decision wasn't a matter for a policy conference or even for permission to implement from higher up. She didn't even think it was enough of an issue to tell anyone about it! By the way, most container/pallets comprise about five percent of the weight of the load—a substantial sum.

The risk the company took in hiring Lisa has surely paid off. For Lisa, too, the job has been positive. I asked Lisa the other day about what this job meant to her. She told me it was great. She said, "Where else can I learn how to run a business? I went to college, but I didn't learn anything about how businesses run."

"What do you mean?"

"Three months ago I had no idea how many pallets would fill a semi-load. And of course it's different if we're talking aluminum or cardboard or glass. I didn't know any of this, but now I do."

Employees can and should make decisions which involve their areas of expertise. When they do, they grow and become more valuable. Python's could set out to find a candidate who already knows all about semi-loads and invoicing, and could even set up ways candidates could demonstrate their skills. Maybe they'd be successful in finding, recruiting, and hiring a candidate with all the knowledge. But by "growing their own" they end up with exactly what they need, custom fit to their situation. When employees have positive attitudes and companies entrust decision making to them, great things can happen.

Growth and continued learning are mandatory. Whether you work for someone else or for yourself, you still work for yourself. There is no job description for an employee like Lisa. In fact, if all that she did in her first three months was ever written down as a list of duties, no one would take the job! She has what it takes, namely, a strong inner source of direction, a strong work ethic, and an attitude which communicates she is willing to do more than the minimum, do whatever is necessary to contribute to her employer.

Is she that special? No. Is she a rare find? I don't think so. But she is employed, moving up, and creating a solid record for herself as a successful, valuable asset.

Behavior that seems consistently positive and pro-ductive is not a result of direction by others, nor is it a reaction to a temporary stimulus. It's the result of using our inner beliefs and values, and expressing our real selves in action. We can live by our values and act consistently with those values any time. We do what Lisa does; we take responsibility for our actions, we value our work, and this is why we are valued.

What builds confidence and self-reliance is what you do with what you have. When Henry David Thoreau wrote, "Being begins in every now," he meant that we can all choose to be positively active today and choose to leave behind the "lives of quiet desperation" he observed that most men lead. Get a job which will allow you to work, to contribute, and to learn and grow. Don't wait for someone to magically bestow upon you the perfect position for which you are ideally qualified. You improvise your career as you go.

Personal investment in your work results in feelings of satisfaction and pride in knowing that you mean something. You've contributed, you have equity, you've done more than accept whatever you're given. Just as you invest yourself in personal relationships, invest yourself in whatever you do to make a living.

People who successfully improvise in their lives know themselves. This is a source of strength, energy, and inexhaustible power that cannot be bought, faked, or ignored. Other attributes of successful people pale in comparison to this one. If you know who you are, you can do anything; and what's more you can enjoy and learn from any job in the world.

Blended Lives

➤ **A blended life means that you use the values** most dear to you to make decisions in all areas of your life.

➤ **Self-control is how we acquire emotional intelligence.** Organizations which can encourage self-control for their members will benefit by working with invested partners.

Chapter Five
Blended Lives

HOW DO WE MOVE from following the prescribed job description enforced by management supervision to a trustful reliance upon the individual's ability to make spontaneous decisions? How do managers and employees change their relationship with each other from the "Do as you're told" mindset to the "Use your own good judgment" mode?

Matching up individual and company values need not be perfect. We don't have to demand that every person's priorities be the same as the company's priorities. It's probably rare if a perfect match exists. But to the extent we can respect the values of the company and commit to our own good judgment, we will probably fare better at work. We must apply individual values to the task of decision making rather than relying upon someone else to decide for

us. What makes this journey worthwhile is the job satisfaction, the pride of self-reliance, and the increase in productivity possible when we express our values through
our work. It is why I look forward to working every day.

Years ago, I don't think I could have made this statement, because my attitude toward my work and my self
was unbalanced. I felt free with my family at home,
enjoyed golfing, an active social life, and other off-work
activities. But I always gave my job first priority. I believed
that since I was the breadwinner in the family, any sacrifice in order to make a living and advance my career was
justified. At one time the loss of my job meant a tremendous loss of my identity. Many people actually believe
their jobs define who they are. Do you? What would happen to your sense of self if you were fired tomorrow?

How individuals integrate their work lives and their private lives has been a key interest to me for years. I've seen
alarming statistics showing vast numbers of employees who
say they don't like their jobs, who feel underemployed,
underappreciated, and underpaid. Job dissatisfaction appears
to be rampant, yet millions of people fear the potential loss
of this miserable employment and choose not to change their
attitudes. I believe that job satisfaction has a whole lot more
to do with what individuals bring to the job and what opportunities for growth and development a company fosters than
what a company might offer an employee in benefits, working conditions, or job guarantees. There are better reasons
to show up for work than just getting a paycheck.

Do you bring your talents, values, effort, and other assets to the job, or do you expect the job to dictate what you should think, feel, and do? Do you invest yourself in the job? If you do, you own your work, and it's as valuable as you make it. If you don't, and you expect the company or someone else to tell you what to do, you're expendable. People are finding out that, after years of training to be compliant and passive, they are no longer marketable. Thinking of our jobs as places we play the entitled role of employee is not productive. It's not valuable to the employer; it doesn't help the company compete.

With family and friends you act spontaneously; you don't hesitate to consider how your actions will further your status or influence your net worth. You send a thank-you note because you are thankful. You pick up a child after school on time because you care about him or her; you don't have to think about it. Thanking a business contact for time spent together and showing up on time for a meeting are behaviors engendered from the same values we readily apply to our personal lives. Why do we consult public relations experts and invest in customer service training seminars to do what most of us know is right? I think it's because we've been trained not to think, to just "do your job."

It's apparent we don't need to be told what to do anymore, nor are we very effective as leaders when we try to tell employees what they should be doing. Employees already know what they should be doing. They need support to do it. They should apply the same good sense they readily express in their personal or social lives to the work they do.

Blended vs. Balanced

Some motivational gurus who have been preaching for us to get our lives in balance have focused on symptoms of dysfunction rather than the problem itself. For instance, experts will attribute problems at home to the fact that someone is working too long and too hard at the office. They'll explain that someone who is not doing well in their job is spending too much time socializing or volunteering in activities not related to the job. Their remedies, since they see the various areas of a person's life out of balance, are to balance the different areas differently. "Spend more time with the family; tell the boss you can't work late again; cut out some of the social activities; get your life in balance," they say.

I suggest a much more realistic model, one which blends areas of your life together, seeking to align areas of your life according to what is most valuable to you. If any aspect of your life is unmanageable, chances are it's not your job's fault, or your family's fault—or anybody's fault. It's just that you are not in control of yourself and the choices you have to make. I believe your life is grounded in an emotional harmony that unites all the areas. There are no such things as family values as distinct from work values or social values. Values are beliefs we choose to act upon. The specific context shouldn't matter.

When we are not acting in accordance with our own values, we suffer pain. This is what makes some people avoid situations they feel might compromise their values. They are avoiding the pain that comes along with that. I've heard people say, for example, "I could never sell just anything. I just couldn't ever get someone to buy something they didn't need or want." Their values make them avoid sales. When we feel guilt or remorse, or when we are sorry about something we've done, we're responding to our sense of values. We decide, for instance, that it's not fair to hurt someone in a business deal, just as it's not fair to hurt a friend or family member. Our values and our actions based upon our values transfer over to all areas of our lives.

Our lives do not equal the sum of separate, departmentalized activities; we only have one life with many kinds of experiences. What is common to all activities in which you participate is you. You can direct all areas of your life in any way you choose. You can simplify your life if you rely upon your values more and think about others' expectations less.

If we act differently in private from how we act in public, the dissonance creates distress, we feel uncomfortable. If we are acting contrary to our values and beliefs, say in a particular social relationship, the relationship will suffer. If we attempt to force our behavior into serving others' values at the expense of our own, we will feel discomfort. I believe we all suffer not from imbalance, which is inevitable, but from alienation from what is most important to us. We do things that are contrary or opposed to our values, sometimes, and justify our willful behavior with false reasons.

Usually we sacrifice what we may feel is best to do for material gain. We do it for the money. Sometimes we act contrary to our natures because we want to avoid conflict or we don't like change. Whatever the excuse, we suffer because we are out of alignment. When things are unblended, they're dysfunctional. This is not to say we can't also be unbalanced, with some areas of our lives receiving no attention and other areas way out of proportion. But the reason for the imbalance is the failure to integrate our values in all areas. I always think it's so sad when people announce they hate their work, or they can't stand their jobs. I believe their problem is not with their job or with their work, but with their disgust for what they've chosen to do.

Play the Real You

When we are acting in harmony with our values, when we are enjoying the relationships in our work as much as our social relationships or family interactions, we are the happiest, and it really doesn't matter much what work we're doing. We are enthused about working. We look forward to being productive. The first test of job satisfaction for anyone should be the same test as the social relationship.

Do you enjoy the company you're keeping? Are you proud of your contribution?

Blending areas of your life means clarifying your values and then making decisions based upon your values. This may mean making some changes, and in some areas these changes may be tougher than others. Leaving a relationship which doesn't fit with our values means we are moving toward health, even though it's painful. Giving up a source of money because it's contrary to our values may be painful, but it can lead us toward a more productive and therefore more profitable career. If you are a different person at home, out with friends, or on the job, examine the legitimacy of your role playing. I think you will find more peace and prosperity in acting according to your own script rather than playing parts written for someone else.

As if to underscore that the time is right for you to begin blending more parts of your life, the workplace no longer supports the scripted actors as it did in the past! Employers want thinking people. They want to hire your creativity and imagination as well as your energy. The message should be clear: the workplace has changed. We have to start making our own decisions, owning our own scripts, and give up the ghost of finding the job that will take care of us. We have to take care of our own business. I have observed that people who do so achieve success both personally and in business. People who are blending their values in their personal and working lives today

are not merely coping with all the changes but are positively thriving in this high-risk, high-tech culture.

For many of us the very nature of our working relationships is changing. The ideas of having employees or
of working for someone else are evolving today into much
more creative and rewarding arrangements. What the
new relationships reflect is a realization that with modern computer and telecommunications technologies,
working together from remote locations is possible as
never before. Home businesses, telecommuting arrangements, and telemarketing businesses are growing incred-
ibly fast today. Our home lives and our work lives are
literally coming together.

The Cindy Sheffield Story

One primary characteristic of those who are wingin'
it is that they see work as an evolutionary process rather
than as a career path. Cindy Sheffield epitomizes such a
person. Back in the seventies, she earned her degree in art
education from the University of Minnesota and taught
art for two years, but she always had an urge to become
involved with sales.

Cindy decided to leave teaching, go on the road, and
sell for a friend who had a custom jewelry business. She
packed her mobile home full of jewelry and was very successful for several months. As with many of us, the trav-
eling began to wear on her. Her father, an insurance
salesman, arranged for her to take a test to see if she

qualified for selling insurance. She didn't pass the test. But because her father had influence, he found an opportunity for her to get started in the business. Her wingin' it skills came into play, and Cindy did very well.

The thought came to her: why don't I sell insurance to groups of individuals? It's probably just as easy to sell to a thousand as it is to sell to one individual. Her first group sale was to one thousand members of a bakers' union in the Twin Cities that represented six different baking companies. She set them up on a benefit plan. Then she realized that no one was set up to keep track of eligibility, process claims, or educate policy holders about the benefits of the program.

It occurred to Cindy that she should start a company to fill this service gap. This was a new idea, so everything had to be created from scratch. Creativity is another primary characteristic of those who are wingin' it. Cindy was very creative in putting this company together.

The operational side of the business was not something that she did very well. Her strength had always been in sales and marketing. She needed someone else.

Those who are wingin' it are always looking for someone to join them and be responsible for a major part of the business. This individual usually has a number of years of experience with other companies and realizes that they would be happier with a leader who practices the art of wingin' it every day.

Julie Harding was the controller of a company that was a client of Sheffield, Olson, and McQueen. Cindy and Julie had an opportunity to work together and found that they had a lot in common, particularly their values. They thought alike in terms of serving their clients and developing their people. Julie had always known her real skill was helping people grow and develop into happy and responsible individuals in their work, so Julie decided to join her as executive vice president and CFO. She has evolved into a leader who is growing and developing key people. Julie, like Cindy, is humble, compassionate, and firm in her work relationships. I asked Julie where her effectiveness came from, and here's the story she told me:

"My parents told us children that it was our responsibility to have respectful relationships with each other. Example: If one of us came to our parents to complain about another, they would say, 'If you're going to point fingers, I'm going to bring all of you together and you will all receive the same punishment.' "

So this is Julie's basic philosophy. A person's responsibility in work is to look after themselves, to focus on their personal growth and development, and not point fingers at others.

Another primary trait of those who are wingin' it is that they accept full responsibility for their relationships. Cindy and Julie don't do strategic planning. They don't have a business plan. They don't have a lengthy job description or a big binder listing policies and procedures. As

Cindy says, "In today's fast-paced world, we've learned by wingin' it together that the quality and competence of the people we hire has more to do with the business growth and success than where you want to go and how you want to do it." So wingin' it is a characteristic of both in terms of the growth and development of Sheffield, Olson, and McQueen.

Twenty-five of their people process work from their homes. Yet another mark of people who are wingin' it is a high level of trust. Both Cindy and Julie have a high level of deep competence, ambition, and trust, the three primary requirements for wingin' it.

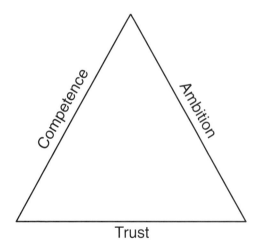

As Cindy says, "We're not conventional in our dress code or in our work rules. Our people are very creative thinkers. We're too busy being who we really are to let ego get in the way."

Both Cindy and Julie are on the track of wingin' it by creating a company where people are trusted, held accountable with consequences, and encouraged to develop their full potential every day.

I asked Cindy, "How do you find competent people, I mean really good people?

She replied with this story: "We were desperate for a receptionist. One day I called 411 to get information and was impressed by the gentleman handling my request. He stuck in my mind. When I called 411 again for information, lo and behold I got this same individual. Again he handled my request so well that I asked him if he was interested in interviewing for a job with our company."

He said, "I'm working right now, but if you give me your name and phone number, I'll call you when I get off work."

Cindy knew right away that this individual had very high values. When they got together again, he was hired. Both Cindy and Julie agree that it's critical how the person answering the phone handles that first call from a customer, prospect, or client. Now they have a professional doing it.

When you're wingin' it together, you make decisions that are right on track with each other. Again, they focus on their people and their relationships. Effective relationships are the number one priority between executives, managers, employees, and customers and suppliers. All things work better when they share mutual respect, trust, and openness.

Good customer relations are a natural by-product of the great relationships inside the organization. Julie says, "We know our work culture is beneficial to the growth of our people. Many competent people have left and then came back."

Julie says that "new people we have hired tell us that our compensation plan matches up well with much bigger companies, and they also like the way we operate. Casual dress, except on dress-up days. Flexible work schedules. Processors can work at home. Mostly, recognition. When a customer writes a letter complimenting an employee, that person is rewarded with fifty dollars. An employee of the month is selected by other employees. They have a monthly drawing called, 'You're the tops.' You are entered by someone you assisted. Managers also have a monthly bonus program based on performance. Our people tell us that the positive recognition they get is very critical to them.

So again, Cindy Olson and Julie Harding are two individuals wingin' it very well together. They have very high standards for themselves and the people in their organization as well as their customers. Cindy Olson, CEO, and Julie Harding, CFO, are a great combination in terms of growing and developing people and teaching the art of wingin' it.

When you're wingin' it, you never achieve perfection. You know that. For example, Cindy and Julie had to make a decision to end a relationship with one of their biggest customers because it was adversely affecting the morale of everyone in the organization. Because they lost significant revenue, they felt they had to lay off thirty people. Well, it was gut wrenching, both for the managers who had to do the layoffs and for Julie and Cindy. But what was amazing was the attitude of the people who were laid off. All of them knew they were competent and they were confident that they would get other jobs, which they did. In fact, they had an unemployment party. They all got together and just enjoyed one another before they parted and went on their different ways.

Sometimes things don't go well. Your attitude and behavior when things go wrong are very important in terms of sustaining relationships with competent people,

At Sheffield, Olson, and McQueen, they have nine people in leadership roles. Each of them is very creative and innovative in developing new ideas to assist their customers and clients. Growing leaders are allowed to make decisions, including who they hire.

Julie said, "We've had some real peaks and valleys over the past eighteen months." They've learned that holding people accountable is okay, and that being too soft is not good for the growth of individuals. People who are wingin' it, who are leaders, understand that individuals do not mind having consequences with accountability as long as they have a clear understanding of what the leader's expectations are. Like Cindy says, "In the past our managers were managed by their people. So then you ask, 'What is the purpose of a manager?'"

They decided that their managers should focus on developing people and that one of the key factors of growth is being held accountable.

Still another earmark of those who are wingin' it: Someone asked Cindy as the CEO to see their business plan, or their five-year plan, and she said, "We didn't have a business plan or a five-year plan when we started and we don't have either of those now. Benefit plans, especially health care, are a rapidly changing business. We found that by being flexible we are able to change quickly and adapt to our customers' needs."

So again, those who are wingin' it don't spend a lot of time talking or thinking about what's going to happen tomorrow or the next day or five years from now. They are too busy adapting and acclimating to the changes taking place right now. Cindy Sheffield and Julie Harding are two of the best I've ever seen at adapting, being flexible, and growing and developing people that provide first class customer service.

Cindy and Julie function about eighty percent of the time with their emotional intelligence. Both of them have very high IQs. They're very intelligent people, but they realize that if they're going to survive in today's highly competitive world of business, particularly in the service business, you have to be creative and innovative. You have to attract competent people and help them grow and develop. And the only way you do that is by building intimate working relationships, first inside the organization with one another, and then outside with customers and suppliers, and that requires emotional intelligence.

Because Cindy and Julie share the same values, principles and standards, they have a tremendous positive influence with everyone that works for them. The key to success, if you're going to be a leader by wingin' it, is that your values, principles, and standards speak louder than your rules and regulations and mandates. Your positive influence on people encourages them to develop to their best potential.

The Receiver Mode— Intensity vs. Effort

➤ **The receiver mode helps us find creative solutions** to problems better than using the computer mode.

➤ **Adopting the receiver mode** requires greater emotional intelligence and self-control.

➤ **We can achieve greater self-control** by eliminating distractions. This enables us to focus positive energy on problem solving and growth.

Chapter Six
The Receiver Mode— Intensity vs. Effort

If you're just coming to grips with a career change or some other transitional point in your life, first establish a healthy state of mind for yourself. Sit down in a silent room and let your mind become quiet. Empty all the anger and anxiety and resentment from your mind. Even if you've been fired and your life is really closing in on you, let all that go and return to that zone which we're all born with. It's a kind of concentration on possibilities, like a peripheral vision in your mind.

Choose Your Thoughts

Allow your mind to think free-flowing thoughts. Some negative ones are going to come into your mind, but don't embrace them. Don't hang on to those; let them go. Don't underestimate the need for this phase. Plenty of alone time is spent replaying old arguments, repeating self-destructive thoughts. Consciously refuse to dwell on any negative issues.

If you refuse to dwell on negative issues, you'll come around to creative ideas. Perhaps it will come after a period of wallowing in self-pity and complaint when the voice in your head says, "Knock it off! You're better than this!" This isn't an easy decision to make, but it is necessary if you want to begin controlling your future. Maybe it will come after you've gone through every cent of savings, you've juggled your bills for months and now your car transmission falls out. Most people need some kind of significant emotional jolt to bring them around to where the cloud of negative self-talk and blaming and self-doubts becomes unacceptable to them, and they willfully see some flickers of something that they think is a good idea.

Suddenly it comes to mind, "Gee, I could do well in the tanning booth business, and people do like to look good, and the sun can hurt them worse than the tanning booth, and I'd enjoy retailing for a change—yeah—and we're in Minnesota and we've got a long winter—yeah, I think maybe I'd like to do that."

"Good. All right, what are you going to do about it?" I'd say to you. Perhaps your private brainstorm may go something like this:

"Well, I need to see where I could buy one or start one, whatever, where would I like to live? Maybe I'd like to live in the town I'm in now. How many tanning booths are there in town now? Who's doing it? Where are they located? What does it cost to put one together?" Do some research. Make sure these things are safe and have a good reputation. Get on the phone. Call the people who make the tanning booths. You know. How much do those things cost? Ask if they help with the financing if you buy a bed from them.

You're starting to improvise; you're wingin' it. You're collecting some information and asking the right questions so you will be able to make a good decision. After studying it, you may arrive at a point where you'll say, "I'm going to do this. I'm going to do the tanning booth. I'm going to put it near downtown. There's a big office where people have time to come out over lunch hour and come in for a couple minutes and get a tan. And the tanning booth company said they would finance it. However, I have to co-sign my house on that one. My mortgage. Yeah, I'm going to do that." And you're on your way!

Creativity comes from a calm, relaxed state; it is not born out of negativism and anger. If you want to find a solution rather than wallow in a problem, force yourself to ignore negative thoughts.

Motivation to Act

You must make a decision to act on what you want in life. A healthy state of mind is the key. Some people need the wake-up call. You see it all the time in health situations; it's called the significant emotional event. Hard-nosed, driven people find out they have a year to live. It's too bad it has to come to this, but when they come out of there, they go through the grieving process. First they're angry and deny the diagnosis and prognosis. Then they're madder than hell because they've got this thing. And they go through bargaining, "God, if you cure me, I'll always be nice; I'll be different." And they go through depression. Finally they reach the acceptance that enables them in most cases to be a different, healthier person. I call this the wake-up call, or in contemporary terms, the change-agent.

They see things differently. They see flowers and grass and rain. They see little kids. Life's great. Darkness is okay. And the moon is beautiful. They start looking at people (who they thought were inept or unproductive before) with compassion and understanding. They start listening to them, and the next thing you know they turn into who they really were all along. They get rid of all that baggage of who they thought they should be, and they know a few new things about themselves.

"Well, I don't have long to live, what does that mean, and who am I going to be? Maybe I'll just be me. For the first time in years, I'm just going to be me." John Donne, the English poet, wrote in his sonnet "Death Be Not Proud," "Death is life's high mede," meaning measure. In other words, without death, life counts for very little. But because of our mortality, every day should be precious. The dying person realizes, "God, I love kids and I love my spouse, and I've got some great friends that I really have let down and I really do like, and I'm gonna get that back. And I really do like to work. I like to do this kind of work."

They commit themselves, "I'm going to do that. I'm going to get a job in sales, and I'm not going to worry about whether I'm the president or the vice president, I'm just going to do that, and I'm going to build the relationships with people, and I'm going to be the best person I can be for whatever time I've got left."

Sometimes just after one of my seminars in which I promote the value of building relationships at work with vendors and customers and co-workers, someone will come up to me and say, "I want to do this but…" Wanting to do something because it makes intellectual sense and committing yourself to act in a certain way because this is a value for you are two different things. People who put the "but" right before "I can't" are too comfortable where they are. For some people, getting fired may be the best thing in the world that can happen to them.

I know, of course, because I have been fired. I am the one who worked long hours right through all my kids' growing-up years, making the money, being the successful business person you see grabbing a quick Rusty Nail or two at the airport bar. I regret the decisions I made that hurt my family and diminished my relationships with my wife and children. But I also act on that regretful attitude. I do invest in my relationships today; in fact, to a great degree my urge to write this book is to help others do the same because I know it's a better way to live.

Here's the important message I really want people to hear: You don't have to wait to be fired to find value in your work life. My suggestion is go back to work. Think carefully about why you're doing this work. Ask yourself some honest questions: What satisfaction does it bring to me? Why do I feel these negative feelings about my work now? Why do I grouse about my boss? Why do I grouse about my co-workers? Why do I grouse about the price or quality of what I'm selling?

I hear a lot of grousing! I say to the complainer, "That's unhealthy. It sounds like you're only doing this for the paycheck. And if that's the case, you're not hurting anybody but yourself because you may not control that paycheck—no matter what you do. All that sacrifice on the altar of expediency will catch up to you. Self-analysis is now in order." It's just a process I'm advocating, but change always involves a loss. Going through introspective, soul-searching processes are necessarily painful.

Go home, become quiet, let the thoughts come in. Who am I? Why am I doing this work? Why am I unhappy about it? What am I going to do about it?

I maintain you don't have to quit. You don't have to wait to be fired. You do have to change your mindset. You have to learn to improvise in your work life whether or not you leave this job. Self-awareness can happen at any age. Your first task is to understand yourself and what you want in life.

Often we try to force solutions upon ourselves. Rather than relaxing and allowing new ideas to surface, we push ourselves and put more pressure on our increasingly limited repertoire of answers. Have you ever tried to remember a name? The harder you try to concentrate, the more remote the name seems to be. Heaping on more distress, more pressure, and more urgency doesn't help. Sometimes, minutes or hours later when relaxed and receptive, the name pops into your consciousness, effortlessly, clearly, and you feel contented. The relaxation mode allows you to be receptive. The tenseness of trying to force your brain to perform seems to have the opposite effect.

Forcing your brain to come up with answers is like using a computer. You know the data is in there; you just have to punch the right keys, and you should be able to call up the data. This computer mode depends upon your IQ more than your EQ. A lot of automatic pieces of information are reproduced in the computer mode, and this computer mode is essential for daily functioning with numbers, language, and memory tasks. But your creativity, problem-solving ability, and relationship skills do not derive from data retrieval. If you have not stored the solution to a problem, you can't remember it. Instead, it is your conscious mind which needs to recombine, imagine, and evaluate various ideas that may work. You must adopt the receiver mode.

Clear your mind and let the natural flow of thoughts occur that contain the answers you need in the present. With the high demands of work today, many of us have difficulty accessing our receiver mode because we are busy doing our jobs. We think we have to take a day off, go on a vacation, or go to a quiet room to clear our minds. Not so. Relaxation means letting go of your need to force yourself. Be easier on yourself. Be humble. Release your tension and distress, and step back from the problem. When you realize the solution will come to you, you can stop chasing it.

When you regain your confidence, it doesn't mean you have the answer, it only means you are receptive and capable of learning. It means you accept who you are, knowing full well you're not perfect. You may be sacred, but you're not a saint! And neither is anyone else. Admit your weaknesses. Practice compassion. Give up defensiveness and the temptations to exaggerate, impress, or make excuses. Start recognizing when you are acting according to one of your values. Let go of the negative self-talk; just stop those comfortable old stereotypical messages. Use the mirror and the smile; get back to who you really are and what you really want and need.

Distractions

The intensity that some people are able to apply to decision making is possible because of an absence of distractions. You see this same intensity in young children. When children play, they typically focus exclusively on their own wants and needs. They get completely absorbed in what they're doing at the moment. Their learning curve is very high when they're so absorbed. They improvise.

Improvising is another way of describing rapid decision making of the kind that keeps you on top of any situation, able to adapt and change to find appropriate solutions.

Improvising is what some children do very well when they create a whole city out of a few building blocks or they make do with a towel as a cape for a superhero's costume. They try new things, modify games, and become very creative because they love what they're doing. This phenomenon of becoming completely absorbed in what you do is a very powerful and productive dynamic in your work. I call it intensity. I see young children able to improvise very effectively because they focus so much on their own enjoyment.

Each of us has intensity, but as adults, we may have to learn to find it. If we can use intensity to direct us, we can improvise more effectively in our work, as kids do in play. The best way to understand intensity is to see it as an absence of distractions. The first step to intensity is to clear your head.

For example, let's say you want to thread a needle. You wet the thread, hold the needle up to the light, and miss the eye of the needle. You try harder and you miss several times in a row. If you stop, clear your mind, and relax, focusing on the eye of the needle, you will be able to thread it. In your work the same focus is required.

Richard worked driving a forklift for a client of mine. He loaded and unloaded pallets. One day he had a lot on his mind; his girlfriend had left him, he'd had a run-in with a co-worker, and he wasn't getting the kind of money and recognition to which he thought he was entitled. Preoccupied, he failed to look in the rearview mirror, and he hit one of the new guys walking behind the forklift. Even though Richard always worked hard, expending a lot of effort, his distractions caused accidents.

Intensity

Many people confuse intensity with effort, but they are two different things. Intensity requires a clear head and relaxation. Effort more often demands we work harder, which puts more pressure on ourselves to work longer hours and maybe pick up the pace even more. This is like constantly adding more power, more force to the situation. More force doesn't necessarily mean more positive results.

Effort and intensity are fundamentally different; for instance, there are three ways to modify the amount of given light you may have. You can increase the amount of energy you put in, perhaps getting seventy-five watts out of a sixty-watt bulb, at the risk of blowing out the bulb. Or you can remove a shade or other veil over the light and you'll achieve a full sixty watts of light from a sixty-watt bulb. Third, you can use a prism or lens to concentrate the sixty-watt light to multiply the amount of light without adding more energy. Removing distractions is necessary to appreciate the increase in light that will result from the lens. Intensifying the light is the same as intensifying your consciousness by first removing distractions and then focusing your mind toward what you want to achieve.

Almost all of the successful people I know do a tremendous amount of productive work in a relatively short time. They seem to be naturally more productive than other people, even though they sometimes spend much less time working. Think of the times you have had work intensity, when you put your whole heart and mind into your work. It was probably fun, and you liked what you were doing. You really "got into it." This applies regardless of the task. Maybe you're envisioning a work project or a model you built or even a closet you finally cleaned out and rearranged. The key is you removed distractions and focused on the task. People who love to read books experience tremendous contentment in being able to concentrate on reading the book.

If it's been a while since you've had that great feeling of accomplishment, what's going on with you? You may have distractions you may not recognize. Some distractions just clutter your mind and take away your focus and enjoyment of what you're doing. One of these distractions is, "How am I doing?" Probably this analytical question wouldn't come up if you were on a roll, doing well. When it does come up, most of us get sidetracked into analyzing motivations and justifying intentions. What sounds like healthy introspection is really a distraction from moving ahead. It doesn't give us satisfaction.

Let's say you're making a third sales call on a prospect who has said no twice before. As you get into your presentation, you don't see a favorable reaction from the prospect. You start thinking, "How am I doing?" This thought takes away from what you are supposed to be doing, which is listening and learning how you can help this prospect. How much you need the sale and all that's riding on whether or not you get the sale are equally debilitating thoughts. If you want to think about what you'll do in the call before the call or after the call, that's okay, but to think about how you are doing while you're doing it is a distraction.

Another distraction which may not look like one is the idea, "Do I like what I'm doing?" "Do I really like being a waitress? or an accountant? or do I enjoy selling?" All of these are selfish self-doubts that sap your energy and effectiveness on the job. Since your being is not equated to your job title, the questions are unanswerable and thus a waste of time. "What else do I have to do?" is the "daily planner" distraction, where you go over and over your schedules and shuffle your planning and make lists, mostly to avoid the task at hand.

Perhaps the most devastating distraction is, "How am I doing in relation to others?" What a waste of time. The more you think about other people's expectations, the more you will be straying from what's really important to you. In other words, please yourself first, and you will always be satisfied! If you listen to your heart, your head will follow.

By harnessing your own intensity and helping others find and maintain more enjoyment in their work, productivity will increase—and errors and burnout should diminish. With intensity, everyone wins. The learning curve is higher when you are focused. Co-workers can count on your productivity rather than contend with your scattered, disjointed activity. And customers win because your performance will exceed their expectations.

Most customer complaints about service people involve a failure to give the customer adequate personal attention. Eliminating those distractions enables you to enjoy the relationship, the opportunity to key in on your customers. The energy you will receive from them will be more positive and reinforcing as well. Work intensity promotes creativity, solves problems, and creates new opportunities for people.

It's amazing what you can do with your career when you bring more intensity to the way you work. In today's high-risk business culture where you may not stay in one job more than four years, your marketability depends on getting things done. The only thing you must do is to quell those distractions, but often this is not easy to do. The real-world, daily deluge of distractions many people tolerate can be very dangerous to entertain.

"Does the boss like me, approve of me, support me?" "I wonder if Shelly and Janice are talking about me?" "Am I doing a good job?" or "Am I doing as well as the new guy?" All these are petty thoughts and phantom problems that distract you. They drag you down into meaningless political issues, social trivia, and counter-productive activity. These issues drag you down because they are beyond your control.

Anything you think and dwell upon that is beyond your control to influence is a distraction to you. I'm not saying that you have to like everything about the job you do (or everybody you work with). I'm saying that dwelling on negative issues or irrelevant activities is probably robbing you of your intensity. If you let yourself be swayed by others' opinions, if you work only to compete so that you can be better than someone else, or if you give your time and energy to things over which you have no control, you will wear out. You'll be more and more unhappy and may even blame your boss, your co-workers or the job itself for your misery.

Discard the rumor mill, organizational politics, and personality differences; these all create distress and waste energy. They never seem to have any closure or resolutions. They exist as distractions for people who do not choose to look toward the future, but who dwell in the drama of the past. You have to control yourself. Get quiet. Clear your head. Stay on task, and invest in your project, your customers, and your family. You can choose to spend your time thinking about strengthening your relationships and learning more about yourself and your skills. If you do find yourself wearing out, remember this: It's not your job that's wearing you out, it's your thinking. You can choose to invest yourself in your work, to learn more, and to develop yourself. You own your work; what it is worth is up to you.

The New Work Order

➤ **Leadership requires positive relationships** between people.

➤ **Leaders serve other employees** by coaching them to accomplish company goals. Part of this support is a responsibility to hold everyone accountable for their work.

➤ **Empowered employees will make good decisions** quickly if they know what they're expected to do.

Chapter Seven
The New Work Order

THE CHANGING ROLE of management is challenging to managers and employees on both personal and professional levels. It's clear that quicker and better decision making is critical to stay competitive today, and I believe people can acquire the ability to make better decisions more quickly if they will clarify their values and work cooperatively with others. Historically, most managers have controlled the dissemination of information to subordinates while trying to control performance by various activity-related measures. Employees today demand more autonomy and respect, and they need much less technical direction.

Managers as Leaders

If you are a manager, you can foster positive relationships with employees by coaching them through their decision making. Employees are just as capable of using their own good judgment as you are, if given the opportunity. To tap into the creativity every person has, first acknowledge and respect the ability every person has for making good decisions. The employee's potential creativity only becomes an asset when he or she uses that creativity to make decisions. The company should become a vehicle to help individuals be more self-reliant so that they can make better decisions more quickly. When everyone is wingin' it successfully, all cylinders are clicking, the business is vibrant and growing, and your competitors will be unable to match your productivity.

Consistent with the supportive role to care for and not caretake employees, the leader's primary responsibility is to understand his or her own attitude and state of mind. The challenge is to remain healthy psychologically, as a leader, while being bombarded with information that complicates making decisions. A leader must also understand and have respect for healthy employee attitudes. A leader must support employees, not dictate to them.

What I see today is high turnover in sales forces, in service industries, and in middle management. There's a tremendous amount of distress, fear, uncertainty, and anxiety, and it's mostly among employed managers. They're scrambling, trying to meet goals and objectives. They're contending with pressure from above to get the job done, get ahead, or get left behind. The quick fix, the quick sale, the quick deal won't do. There is another way to work, and it's much more productive.

An alternative to all this frenetic "busyness" might be to quiet down. Calm yourself. Hire the very best people you can who have the very best attitude about themselves. If their attitude about themselves is good, and they feel good about themselves, the likelihood of working effectively with the group is better. And then the likelihood of working with clients and customers is better. Give them all the relevant information they need to make good decisions fast. Give up that omniscient, analytic role; adopt a supportive, coaching role.

#1 Marketing Advantage: Relationships

The ability to develop good relationships is the secret to success in American business. This is especially true of the frontline sales or service areas where millions of people are employed. Companies still need a president who has a vision and investors and boards of directors who will keep the company moving forward. You need a controller of a company who understands finance. You need a research and development department that will create new ideas and concepts. When you get into the area of selling, the business world has changed dramatically. It's still true that "nothing happens till someone sells something," but who makes the sale is increasingly more a matter of personality. Products can't "sell themselves"; the buyers are too sophisticated today. Promotional words such as "new, improved, best, lite, free, giant, and natural" just don't mean anything. Real product or service differentiation and advantage are achieved by making a personal connection with the buyer.

The customer rarely sees top management. Salespeople and service providers have to do more for the customer than just take orders or supply minimal attention. Today most customers can make their own orders from a catalog, a mailing list, an Internet address, or over the phone. Self-service is always going to be cheaper for the customer, so service providers are challenged to provide more value. This is where relationships come in and where businesses can obtain unbeatable advantages over competitors.

Besides cementing long-term customer loyalty, salespeople and service providers who are treated with respect and who are empowered to create or improve products or services can energize a company. The manager's primary role today is to make good decisions quickly and empower co-workers to do the same by supporting their growth and development through relationship building. Employees will treat customers much the same way they themselves are treated.

My salespeople were actually charged with one thing and one thing only: to build the relationship with the customer. When my salespeople completed an interaction with a client, they recorded on tape the essence of the call; for instance, if the client bought anything, needed more information, or had any particular requests, the salesperson would record the message. The salesperson also would state what the next action step or follow-up should be. That went into the file. So if the particular salesperson was out for a period of time on vacation or whatever, and if someone had to fill in for him or her, the file was there. They knew when the last call was made. They knew what went on with that call. We had a system of keeping track of the interaction with the client because we believed that was critical.

I think that salespeople should want to do more than sell radio time, do more than sell ads. I encourage them that if they're going to call on an outdoor power equipment distributor, for example, they should know a lot about their prospect's outdoor power equipment business. I think a salesperson should take some time to research and learn about the industry, the company, and the possibilities of working together. By learning something about the prospect's business, you not only grow in your perspective, but you should certainly exceed the prospect's expectations regarding most salespeople.

You should go another step beyond. I had a salesperson, Billy Weir, who was very successful in the outdoor power equipment market. He studied other people in the business who appeared to be more successful than his prospect. He'd say to the prospect, "Listen, I did a little research. There's a guy down in Des Moines who has a distributorship for Cadet tractors, and he's doing some things with his dealers that are quite extraordinary. He's got a program where he will come in and train the dealer's salespeople in their own store. The distributor provides a trainer for a two-hour program on how to sell the Cadet brand. What's happening is these dealers are featuring Cadets instead of Toros in the front row, and they're moving like hotcakes. I just thought I'd share that with you."

"Well, that's a great idea, we ought to do that here." Now the radio ad salesperson has become a consultant, an information source. "It seems like every time you call on me, you're telling me something new."

The salesperson replies, "Well, yeah, I'm very interested in your business."

You build a relationship and you position yourself. You're positioning yourself with these people as being different from the average salesperson who's calling on them. You bring them a perspective they need to stay competitive; you add value to your relationship. But first you added value to yourself. You researched, you learned, you became an expert. Would you say by this example that this salesperson was just mouthing the company line, or was he an individual making a sale on behalf of the company? Which kind of salesman would you hire?

There's no way you could force a salesperson to actually go to a library or call up suppliers and find out the information Billy Weir found on his own. It's just not part of any job description I've ever seen. But what you can do is establish for Billy the principle of doing business by giving value. You'll be pleased if you're the sales manager and Billy lands this account. But you'll really value Billy if his relationship with the client means more ads in the future. This is the kind of relationship companies need to cultivate with their salespeople.

Some entrepreneurs have a tough time when their business begins to become successful. Their personal sales start to climb, and they begin to stretch their supply lines, so to speak, and they end up trying to do the million things that it takes to run a company all by themselves. But growth, success, and expansion bring with them the inevitable need to build relationships with others who will work with them. Let's imagine you're the business owner, trying to expand your business.

Working with People

Getting people to work *with* you is the key concept here, as opposed to working *for* you. The salesperson who can only promote the features and benefits of whatever you're selling, for instance, works *for* you. Someone like Billy Weir works *with* you. I'm not suggesting that you make every employee a full partner, but the popular trends in employee relations, namely, more Employee Stock Ownership Plans (ESOPS), more profit-sharing schemes, more employee concessions in return for more representation on boards of directors, do express an essential reality of work relations today.

Stop here and ask yourself, "Which has more appeal to me? To work *for* somebody? Or do I prefer to be working *with* somebody?" If someone is working *with* you, he or she has a sense of sharing in the successful growth of the enterprise. If you are hiring people to work *for* you, they tend to feel like dependents who have little sense of control of their own destiny.

No one wants to work *for* anybody! People want to work for their own reasons: their own growth, development, profit, and so forth. This doesn't mean everyone wants to own a company, but everyone wants to own their own work, and the wise employer knows this and asks for a partner, not a peon.

The leveling of the company hierarchies is being forced by economics and competition, but the result is an acknowledgment that everyone must be more responsible for their own production. Perhaps the bottom layers of the work force have also evolved educationally to the point where they are unsatisfied unless they are given the opportunity to make their own decisions, just like management. The most immediate revelation of this parity is that managers and employees share the same emotional, psychological, and motivational needs. Although perhaps shocking for many traditional managers, most employees have always known this to be true.

When managers admit they're fallible and vulnerable to the same ups and downs in moods and competence as everyone else, uneasy fears about their loss of authority and the breakdown of the secure hierarchy almost always surface, especially among veteran managers. When people in management begin a healthy self-examination, they almost always fear a loss of control, and they may feel threatened and become defensive as well. This is a natural response to perceived changes in role expectations.

I have no qualms about hierarchy. What I have qualms about is when it becomes dictatorship or a caretaking protectorate. Hierarchy is okay. There's the boss. There's his or her associate. And there's the manager. I've worked for and reported to lots of managers in my careers. I've reported to a lot of presidents. All this positioning is fine with me, and probably necessary and worthy of respect. How well the relationship with subordinates works is the critical factor.

When you see the president, how does he or she communicate with you? "Hi Don, good to see you again." Or does the president walk by and not say anything. And then does his or her next in command walk by and ignore you? Whenever this happens, you don't feel a part of the company. You're alienated by this arrogant attitude, and I maintain it's wrapped up with some kind of make-believe aura of infallibility, as pompous and arrogant as the emperor who had no clothes.

While I was walking with the president of a manufacturing company in his 150,000-square-foot plant in Rogers, Minnesota, I witnessed a casual encounter that illustrates how easy it is to establish rapport. He encountered a maintenance worker. In front of thirty or forty guys the boss says, "Hey, give me five!" to the maintenance man and slaps his hand. "Give me five, great job, you keep this place spic and span and I appreciate it." And we kept on walking.

This man understands his employees, and he knows how to show his appreciation for what they do. What better recognition is there than a public display of sincere appreciation? We're not talking about a monthly review/ personnel appraisal system. We don't have to institutionalize a merit program. We just have to be aware when others are doing a good job and thank them once in a while. This man understands what really motivates people: honest, sincere recognition—a high five in front of our peers. Working positively, and respectfully *with* employees is the goal of the new work order.

Empowerment

Many people espousing empowerment and team-building ideas don't understand how to empower. They think that just by telling people, "I'm now going to empower you; now you make decisions," that they are modern day Lincolns, and that the freed will suddenly respond by working overtime to make good decisions! Some people want empowerment like they want major surgery. I say this not to be cynical, but because empowerment means making decisions. It means change. When you hear, "I'd rather not, thank you very much!" don't give up on the wisdom of empowering people to make their own decisions.

As the leader, if you really want your employees to make decisions, then you'll have to build relationships with them. You'll also have to make sure they know the values that are most important to the company. This incident happened at the business of one of my clients, Grand View Lodge, and it illustrates how actions flow from values and how companies can benefit from encouraging individuals to do what is right.

A guest came up to the front desk and asked where he could buy shaving cream, toothpaste, and other toiletries; he had forgotten his kit. The counter person told him they didn't stock those things, but asked what brands of shaving cream and toothpaste he preferred. She said she'd get back to him. She asked an associate to take care of the front desk. She drove three miles away to the store, and purchased the items he needed, including an inexpensive shave kit. She then delivered the items to the guest's cabin, no charge. She was honored by her supervisor and her co-workers for making a great decision.

Another example of remarkable initiative involved one of the grounds crew at Grand View. The par four fifth hole at the Pines has water in front. A player tried to hit a wedge about ninety yards to the green over the water. He hit three balls into the water and then hurled his wedge into the water. He and his fellow players tried to retrieve it, with no success, and moved on to the next hole. The grounds crew person drove his tractor to the main shed, changed into his bathing suit, and swam out into the water.

It took him twenty minutes to find the club. He changed back into his work clothes and took one of the golf carts to the seventh hole, where he presented the player with his wedge.

This young man has a high degree of emotional intelligence. He saw the innocence in the actions of the golfer, he felt compassion for him and acted automatically to assist him with his problem. When you have a strong sense of values and the organization supports your initiative, humility and compassion triumph over arrogance and indifference. People want to serve others without being subservient. The crew person was heard to say, "It was worth the swim to see the look of surprise and hear his words of gratitude when I handed him that wedge."

The healthy culture respects the potential of every person, and the wise company strives to get the most out of people. When we hear of companies laying off hundreds or thousands of people, we should be concerned; it's a tragedy for those being let go, but it's also shamefully expedient. It's apparent the value of people in these corporations has been calculated not on their actual or potential capabilities but on their dysfunctional performance, not on their ability but on the inability of the corporation to obtain productivity. This is like trashing a car which goes only twenty miles per hour while failing to acknowledge you never shift into second gear! By the way, if you buy another car, maybe even a shinier model, and you fail to shift gears into second, you'll still only hit about twenty miles per hour!

This distinction in the work relationship is very important because people do or don't do well depending upon their willingness to do their best. Companies that can manage to harness individual commitment and productivity thrive. Those that treat people like slaves get minimal compliance and a lot of sabotage. So *with* is a very important relationship: it's inclusive, it's partnering, it's appealing to everyone's sense of pride. Working with others means we build intimate relationships. We have compassion for others, even as we acknowledge our own imperfections.

It feels good to have compassion toward other people. A higher degree of understanding about them and the complexities of how they're dealing with situations makes you more human. Because of how you're conducting yourself, you become more calm. You make quick decisions. You do it in a manner that's relaxing. And others like your decisiveness, and respect you for your sincerity.

When you show you understand someone else, when you're honest with them, other people will want to emulate you. All it takes is a conscious shift in thought for a leader to believe and say to employees, "You've had years of experience, and you probably know a lot about how to get this work done well. You should make these decisions. I'll support your efforts. If you use your intuition, your common sense, based on your experience, I think you'll make good decisions." We know our roles are to support people, require accountability, and redirect those that have problems with performance. We understand the value of compassion, fairness, and intimacy in all relationships; this is the new work order.

Rapport

➤ **Humility, Compassion, and Intimacy** are characteristics emotionally mature people and successful organizations have in common.

➤ **A way to learn and grow** is to build relationships with all kinds of people.

Chapter Eight

Rapport

IN THE BUSINESS WORLD some of us have become fixated on impersonal, objective events that are supposed to indicate success. We measure growth by the size of our companies, staffs, market, or capacity. We track profit margins, market share, or price to earnings ratios. Efficiency experts and the activity managers apply their talents to manipulate events to influence the measurements that are supposed to tell how well the company is doing. These logical, left-brained, linear measures do not show the whole picture. It's like using an IQ score to judge the worth of a person.

For employees in general, most of the statistical business measures are largely irrelevant. It is only natural to care most about what you own, your vested interest, or what you control. Most employees don't own the company. Even taking into account the most loyal of employees, the participants in stock ownership or profit-sharing plans, employees still don't make the major policy decisions. They contribute, they're a part, they're vital to the mission, but they don't own the company. It is natural, then, that they are more interested in what they do own, have a vested interest in, and do control—and that's their work.

Individuals care more about their personal growth and development than they do about the company. If they see the company as a way for them to progress, they'll be more loyal. If they see the company as an impediment to their own growth, they'll spend their energies elsewhere. This is not a response to any particular philosophical or management theory; this is the way it is, and it's natural, just as rivers run downstream. The best part about this realization for companies is that helping individuals grow and mature also increases their asset value for the company. Even the most linear-thinking, hard-nosed economist should recognize that when you increase the productivity of the worker, you increase the productivity of the company. The equity of a company is not a number which relates to what a company has produced, but rather it describes its potential productivity if all personnel gave everything they had.

If the statistics about activity and other performance data are not sufficient to judge the success of a business, what do we use? How do we measure how much of a company's capacity is actually being achieved? Some people will say you can't measure good will, reputation, capacity for growth, creativity, and a myriad of other "intangible" assets. But you can.

Profitability, longevity, and growth will not be achieved without these assets. The excellent companies profiled in the business books and held up as models all have an abundance of these assets. Although the meanings change a little when applied to a business entity like a company or a corporation, the characteristics of humility, compassion, and intimacy can apply to people and organizations. These are not your typical corporate images. But they are the characteristics that help people and organizations be most effective, especially when they're under pressure. How do these characteristics fit into how you and your company operate every day?

Humility, Compassion, and Intimacy

One who has humility or is humble is realistic. Rather than pretending some sort of superiority, we all should acknowledge reality and act accordingly. People who have humility build trustful relationships; they're approachable; they're predictable. Predictability is good in business. It carries a high value because of a lower risk of disappointment and uncertainty. The company which is humble knows it doesn't have to exaggerate claims, try to own the world market, or cut down competitors in order to boost its image. The company with humility is still learning from its customers how best to meet their needs.

Like humility, compassion is sometimes viewed as a weakness, but it is truly just the opposite. Compassion means you can relate to another's situation. All the advice on how to deliver good customer service, whomever you define your customer to be, starts with understanding the customer's point of view. This is compassion. Everyone in business is someone's customer, both inside and outside of the company. Understanding each other's predicaments and strengths is important in building trustful relationships. It also makes work a place where you care for other people and they care for you. How do you think this dimension impacts productivity?

Finally, intimacy, as we discussed earlier, is the ability to be the same person at work that you are off the job; to blend your values into all areas of your life. You relate to everybody with respect; you don't stand on ceremony. Intimacy means you give your best because you've promised to do so.

Of course, intimacy usually refers to personal relationships that may not require high maintenance but remain trusting. George Pransky loved to talk about intimacy, particularly with men, guys in their fifties, who've been running companies. He'd start seminars with, "What we're going to do today is become intimate." He said, "I love to watch their faces."

"We're what?"

Interpersonal intimacy is about listening for feeling, not content. Intimacy is about listening to understand, not to reply. Intimacy is about building instant rapport with people, because you radiate the warmth and understanding that everyone is looking for. Intimacy is really the key to opening relationships. It's also the key to building and sustaining relationships. With intimacy in a personal relationship, for instance, you can do almost anything, and it will be fun to do: you can go to a movie, you can walk in the rain, take a canoe ride, go fishing. Or go to the queen's ball. It's fun because you have intimacy. He said this is what is needed in the workplace. People are dying for intimacy in their jobs, this feeling of warmth and understanding with the people they work with and the people they report to. Work's no fun without it.

Humility, compassion, and intimacy can rehumanize your business. These are the experiences that are really important to individuals. Corporate leaders who can unite people and pull them forward by tapping into these essential needs will have less turnover in the work force, more loyalty, more productivity, and more pleasure both in relating to others on a positive level and encouraging others to grow. Companies can cultivate these characteristics in the way they relate to their customers as well. Not many, but a few businesses make you, the customer, feel like one of the family.

Do you love your auto mechanic? I love my auto mechanic. My wife loves our auto mechanic. Stevie Haglund was a mechanic in the Amoco Station in Buffalo, one of the back-room guys. For a lot of us bringing the car to a service station is a negative experience. Most people are suspicious of auto mechanics. Watch them very carefully, we say to ourselves, because they're never going to do it right. If they say they're going to change your oil and filter, of course they'll leave the old oil filter in and charge you just the same. Stevie Haglund proves that relationships are really the key to business success.

The moment you meet Stevie you know he has integrity. You seem to recognize his sense of values, and you feel you can trust him implicitly. When people do things the way they say they're going to be done, you begin to trust. I came into his shop one day and said, "I've got this funny noise in the brakes, and I may need new brakes—" What an opening! I came back an hour later, and he said, "It was a little sand in the brake drum, and I had to smooth it down a little bit." He said, "That'll be ten bucks." He could have done a four-hundred-dollar brake job. In my mind the brakes were shot. I even told him I thought they were gone.

I trust him so much that I have given him tons of openings over the years, and he never has taken advantage. My wife and I and many others remember, and we constantly refer people to him, our good friends and relatives in particular. We want them to experience an auto mechanic who has integrity. When Stevie decided to start his own service center, he bought an old building in town, and all of us who knew him at the Amoco immediately went with him over there. He had one hundred customers right off the bat. He's really dedicated himself and committed himself and his employees to have the finest auto service center in Buffalo.

By the way, he doesn't sit in the office; he's the master mechanic. He oversees everything and serves as the example for his employees. He still has dirty hands. He still interacts with customers. Stevie is an example of someone who is wingin' it successfully. He makes hundreds of decisions daily. His decisions are fast and his decisions are right.

Make Friends

Successful entrepreneurs, homemakers, salespeople, artists, and people in every other endeavor make things happen; their passion manifests itself in action. They "do." They're proactive. These are all the characteristics of leaders who want to control their environment, to shape their own future. These doers are the ones who live the old coaches' slogan: "If it's to be, it's up to me." But this doesn't mean they achieve great things alone.

In fact, it is only through relationships that we can grow beyond where we are, reach beyond our limitations, and multiply ourselves. As technology, automation, and instant access to information increase competition worldwide, relationships are the only edge you will have today in any business category.

Other people are important. Each of us knows how good it feels to be treated as an important, contributing person. Unfortunately we also know how it feels to be disrespected and discounted. Acknowledging others' value means we will assume others want what we want and need what we also need. It is a kind of mature attitude that has nothing to do with age, and everything to do with forging relationships.

I have the habit in restaurants of establishing rapport with the wait staff. I want to connect with my waitperson, find out a little about him or her. Why? Because I recognize his or her worth. I want to give a little, acknowledge him or her as a person. If I can build a certain rapport with the waitperson, the relationship can continue throughout the time I'm in the restaurant. If the waitperson really enjoys what he or she is doing, I have a better lunch!

One experience I recall involved Sally. She kept coming back saying, "More ice tea?"

I said, "You do an extraordinary job; you must really enjoy this work."

"Right, I do."

And I said, "Why did you choose waitressing?"

"Well, the variety of things you get to do every day and quite frankly, if you do what I do the way I do it, the tips are real good. And I enjoy it. I enjoy making people happy while they're eating. I love it."

That's kind of neat. Now, is that "Waitress Sally Jones?" No, that's Sally Jones being a waitress. I like to connect with people like Sally because she affirms my belief that there is nobility, worth, and tremendous inspiration in everybody. I'm certainly not Will Rogers in that I can't truthfully say, "I never met a man I didn't like," but I will go to my grave insisting people are fundamentally good, that every person has a valuable lesson to teach, and that we all miss so much in life by discounting or ignoring other people's worth. The greatest impediment to acquiring wisdom in my view is the conviction that you know more than everybody else!

In the middle sixties I built a radio station in Brainerd, Minnesota, with two partners. As the general manager, I found that doing everything myself was an exhilarating challenge, but I knew I had to surround myself with good people, and I don't mean just good employees. The way I saw it, I had to connect with community business people so that they would support my station. I knew what a good radio station should have, and I wanted to build long-term advertising support. In the radio business, your market is pretty well defined by the strength of your signal, and within that broadcast area, you have to know both your listeners and your sponsors very well.

I was the morning announcer. I signed the station on at 5:00 A.M., and I was on the air four hours till 9:00 AM. After this shift was an opportune time for me to connect with business people who would listen to me doing my schtick in the morning show. When I'd get off the air, I'd go home, shave, put on my business suit, and I'd call on a prospect such as Bob Brecken from Brecken's Store. Bob would say, "That was kind of a corny joke you did this morning."

I'd reply, "Bob, do you have a better one? I'll use it tomorrow morning." I had this instant rapport on a sales call because they'd all heard me.

I wasn't making a cold call, I was making a warm call. The guy at the auto dealership had heard me on the radio, and then he'd see me in person, and he always would say something about the voice. I remember Bud Henderson, Viking Tire, a General Tire dealer. When I first called on him, he said, "So this is Don Wohlenhaus, come on in!"

Establishing rapport is so important that it's usually the first chapter in most sales books. Other business coaches will talk about developing the trust relationship or the consultative sales approach. They advise you to establish the partner to partner relationship with a prospect. They talk about treating your prospect, customer, or client as a person. They believe in, "Do unto others as you would like them to do unto you." I would add: be interested in the individual for his or her own sake, not just for what the person can do for you.

It's easy to make the case that customers are more likely to buy from you if they like you and there is mutual respect. But the measure of your success is not if you get the sale, but rather if you develop a relationship or learn something or share something. To feign interest as some sort of sales step is dishonest and disingenuous. Of course, positive relationships make for more business success, but positive relationships are much more important than mere business success because they help us all grow, mature, and become more compassionate.

Most of our values derive from the lessons we have learned through experiences with people who care about us. Our role models, mentors, heroes, and teachers all discovered ways to relate to us, to show us the way, and to give us confidence. We then take their lessons and use them in our own modeling, teaching, and influencing other people. Who bothered to establish rapport with you?

Learn From Other People

People talk about the lack of heroes today. The commercialization and marketing of famous people seem to ignore so many old-fashioned values. People complain that youth today have no role models. I'm not that concerned. Albert Schweitzer wasn't as important to me as an eighty-year-old Polish neighbor-lady who taught me to make soup when I was five. The apparent absence of national heroes is no more devastating than the absence of parents, neighborhoods, and youth clubs. We learn from ordinary people close to us. This is also true in business.

Harry Stanius is one of my mentors. I've known him for about twenty-five years. He's my role model for life. He has brown eyes and a very kind, warm, and reassuring face. His expression always suggests a quiet kind of confidence. And he's a good golfer. In fact, at the St. Cloud Country Club, when you chip in from thirty feet or when you sink a sixty-foot putt, it's called a "Stanius." He's got incredible confidence, but it's more than luck. He's been practicing chipping and putting for decades. Harry is a good model for someone who is wingin' it all the time. He and his wife, Sue, run The Camera Shop in St. Cloud.

It's a wonder how Harry did so well during the seventies and eighties, when literally hundreds of "ma and pa" camera shops went out of business in this country. Harry not only survived, he prospered and is now expanding. There are lots of reasons for his success that have nothing to do with luck. Everyone knows Harry. His shop radiates warm feelings. Harry is the reason the shop succeeds, and by looking at his particular style of relating to people, I have learned better how to relate to other people myself. He literally passes on his self-confidence and compassion for others to everyone he meets. He's always satisfied all of my needs, and never have I found him unable to answer a question. He exceeds everyone's expectations.

I was in his shop one day when a couple of teenagers walked in. They were a little scrubby looking, not what one would call the ideal prospects. He broke off our conversation and went over and treated them with the utmost respect and tremendous consideration; his intensity in trying to serve them impressed me greatly.

They asked him a lot of tough questions—I had no idea what they were talking about. He answered all their questions, and I could tell that after a little while the young man just started melting. I mean when he came in he was kind of rigid, harsh. But after interacting with Harry for a few minutes I could see him leaning forward, leaning in on the counter, listening intently, nodding his head. Harry was patiently explaining how to make a negative better, showing how to re-do a picture to improve it, enlarge it, and so forth.

The young man said he was only in town for a short period, couldn't come back, had things to do, and asked how long it would take to fix his prints. Harry paused and said, "How about thirty minutes?" There was nothing else to say—the customer just looked stunned and smiled. Throughout the whole interaction, Harry never wavered in his intense listening, and he focused only on the customer's needs. This is Harry, and he's like this with everybody. Whether you're a banker or president or two scrubby young people who arrive in a beat-up pickup truck, you're going to be treated with compassion and respect at Harry's store.

He's the role model for his employees. One day I saw one of his employees having a hard time with a customer. Harry ambled over and put his hand on the employee's shoulder and said to the customer, "You must be having a real challenge here, is there something I can help you with?" It disarmed the customer, and the employee's tension just faded away.

When the customer left, Harry said to his employee, "Okay, have compassion. You know that person was probably having a bad day. They're a little insecure, a little out of balance." He paused and the employee nodded, resigned to giving the customer the benefit of the doubt. Harry continued, "So our role is to try and take that into consideration. I know it's hard, but if you do that, it's good for you. You'll feel better. Don't let that customer's attitude ruin your day."

People such as Harry are always guided by an ability to make good decisions. I have given a lot of thought to what motivates them to act with compassion and respect for others. The exceptional customer service Harry displayed was not put on, nor was it some learned sales technique he picked up at a seminar. Harry is the same with me in or out of the store.

Harry is also my golfing partner. He taught me the rules, but even more, he taught me to play by the rules. The first rule is to follow the rules even when no one is watching—don't move the ball around. Don't take extra strokes. Respect the rules as you respect yourself. As a metaphor for life, he believes in absolutes. Cheating in golf is chipping away a piece of yourself every time. Playing by the rules is Harry's life. I use Harry as an example of someone who blends different parts of his life together, welded by common values in practice.

The rules for him and the values I refer to that guide an individual's conduct or a company's policy making are really all the same ethic. I love Stephen Covey's work. His *Seven Habits of Highly Effective People* has influenced thousands of people. What do you believe in? What's most important? He makes the convincing case that relationships are very important and there are seven things that you should do or think of doing to be truly effective in your life. I just don't think it's seven things, I think it's one thing—act on your values.

In a very tangible way, relationships in my careers have helped me develop the confidence I now have, have given me models of behavior, and have been the most important aspects of my life in business. Learning from relationships, however, is not limited to learning from only good, nurturing experiences. Sometimes your best moments in life precede or follow some of the most dire disappointments.

I was vice president of Fuller Laboratories when the company was sold to Parke-Davis. Dick McCarthy, the

CEO of the company and one of my lifetime mentors, took me in his office, sat me down, and said, "What do you plan on doing? You know, you could keep a job with Parke-Davis who bought the company."

I replied, "Dick, I don't want to do that, I really don't."

He continued, "Why don't you think about what you want to do."

And I said, "I think I'm going to buy a radio station."

"Oh, well, good," he said, "when you get that all put together, come and talk to me, I'd like to hear about that."

I left the company, but less than two years later I decided to buy a radio station in Buffalo, Minnesota. The price tag was right, about three hundred thousand dollars. But the bad part was that I needed sixty thousand dollars down which I did not have. So I went to Dick and told him all about this situation. He said, "How are you set financially?"

I said, "Well, that's the bug, I need this money." And so on.

And he said, "How much do you need?"

I said, "I've been able to raise thirty thousand dollars, so I need thirty thousand dollars more, but I don't know where to get it."

And he said, "Okay." He opened his drawer and he took out his checkbook and he wrote me a check for thirty thousand dollars, and then he took out a little piece of paper and in his own handwriting he wrote, "This is a note between Richard M. McCarthy and Donald Wohlen-haus. It's for interest only. The interest will be five percent for as long as you need this money." So he gave me thirty thousand dollars interest only, at five percent for as long as I needed the money. And I signed it. And he handed me the check. That was a real lesson. I mean, I broke down a little bit on that one. I said, "Dick, I can't tell you—"

And he cut me off, "Let me tell you, as you travel through life, you will have an occasion to help someone as I'm helping you. Do it." That's all he said.

By the way, as time went along out there west of the Twin Cities in Buffalo, things were going very, very well, and through the seventies the interest rates went up. I automatically increased the interest from five to seven to eight to nine to ten percent over a period of six years, without being asked, because I knew that was the market rate. I bring this up not to flaunt my sense of integrity, but to reemphasize that this was not just a great business deal— that it would be wrong to take advantage of someone, particularly someone who had helped me. I could have kept the interest at five percent. When the chips are down, it's relationships that count.

Pinches, Crunches,
and Moods

➤ **Caretaking is destructive to relationships;** leaders care for people by supporting their growth and development.

➤ **Pinches are unmet expectations;** crunches are accumulated pinches. Negotiate expectations.

➤ **Moods are.**

➤ **Leadership functions** within relationships, not in theory.

Chapter Nine
Pinches, Crunches, and Moods

I have had people in my life care enough about me that they helped me when I needed their help. Dick McCarthy, Larry Haeg, Sr., and Ken Light all cared for me. I call them my mentors. Now I find myself in the role of a mentor in my consulting practice, and as I care for my clients and want to help them solve personnel problems, I constantly run into companies that seem to be stuck in the caretaking mode.

Caring For vs. Caretaking

Recently a client in the retail business told me he just plain didn't like his employees. He thought they were lazy malingerers who dedicated themselves to stealing his peace of mind. He told me stories about his employees stealing things, about their tardiness, poor customer service skills, and the outrageous workers compensation and wrongful discharge lawsuits he had endured. He talked about his frustration at being unable to recruit and hire a better class of worker. Not surprisingly, his attitude was not difficult to detect; in fact, every employee knew exactly what he thought. For this manager to ever improve his effectiveness as a leader, he first had to acknowledge that his attitude was part of the problem. I feel for his predicament, for many managers, like many teachers and parents, somewhere learned the message that they should do everything for their employees, students, and children.

You can certainly prefer to socialize with other people than your employees, and you certainly have a right to disapprove of negative performance. But what is suicidal is to assume that others are incompetent or somehow morally or ethically defective, or to conclude that people want to fail because they do not perform the way you'd like them to.

A substantial number of managers I work with blame their employees to some degree for their company's problems. Not only is this not productive or in any way remedial, but it clouds the real issues which could make for a healthier working relationship. The negative attitude toward employees is usually the result of a caretaking manager, a caretaking company, and a caretaking culture that attempt to control their work through various manipulative tactics.

Caretaking masquerades as concern for someone, but it is actually contempt in disguise. A certain arrogance underlies most caretaking. When employee performance falls short of expectations and employees are not held accountable, that's caretaking. When the frustrated manager takes over and does the job him- or herself, that's caretaking. When expectations are lowered or the standards are compromised, that's caretaking. When excuses are more acceptable than confronting problems and finding solutions, that's caretaking. Trying to manipulate employee performance, mostly with the carrot and/or stick approach, is caretaking.

One problem with caretaking is that it doesn't work. Often it backfires. The more you bribe and threaten, the less return you get. The more you try to control and manipulate the work, the less investment the employee has in the outcome. An inherent lack of respect and trust accompanies most caretaking, whether it's done by parents, spouses, or bosses. A legitimate measure of a manager's skill and professionalism is the degree to which he or she avoids caretaking other people. What makes caretaking so dangerous is that it passes for concern. It is justified by expediency. Always the caretaker can claim status as a martyr, or one who gives beyond the call of duty. But the end result is most always disappointment, resentment, and frustration; after all, work is not being done.

The better model for working with other people is the "caring-for" model. The goal of caring for someone is not to manipulate their work, but to provide whatever support you can to help them to do their best. This relationship doesn't seek to manipulate—it seeks to empower. The assumption (value) is that others are perfectly capable of the performance. Business leaders should see themselves more as coaches. Some coaches have a wonderful ability to inspire, motivate, and give their players confidence. Their role is to help the players learn and grow and play up to their potential; the coaches themselves will never take the field. Literally, they can't do it for their players.

To get more, employers should establish intimate, trusting relationships with employees, and employees should be willing to invest themselves in the business. If this arrangement sounds a little like marriage counseling, it's no wonder to me. It makes perfect sense to me that you should expect people with whom you work to care about you, and that your bosses should expect your best efforts, just like expectations in a personal relationship.

I'm convinced that it is necessary that every member of the work force participate in decision making to some degree. When the decision involves you, you should have a say. I am also aware this is a tremendous shift in the operating style of many companies. People do not suddenly change within a system, even if the system has committed to change, and the leadership needs to show the way by first changing its relationship to employees from supervisor to coach, and from monitor to troubleshooter. Leaders dealing with individuals who may not feel very confident about making decisions must be absolutely committed to building that individual's confidence by caring for him or her and not caretaking the employee.

When I preach to leaders that they should be aware of employees' moods and where they are in the grieving process as it relates to change and empowerment, it can sound kind of soft and fuzzy, I know. But this isn't meant to put managers in the roles of psychiatrists or to make excuses for poor employee performance. As a leader, you should count on and respect the integrity of your employees. Insist on accountability and responsibility. If you are the employee, take pride in doing what you say you will do. Take advantage of all opportunities to work and do your best.

We need to understand the caring-for model. I might tell an employee, "I care for you as an individual. I understand that, like me, you have moods, and sometimes you're going to be up and sometimes you're going to be medium and sometimes you're going to be down. But I also understand that when I hired you, you said you wanted to work here. You were willing to commit yourself to whatever responsibilities we agreed upon."

You may be hired to drive the products of a company to the consumer. That's what you'd do as a marketing director, or as a salesperson, for instance. That has to be done. In the broadcast advertising business, my conversations between my salespeople about sales goals or targets went something like this:

Now, I'm not going to tell you how to make this sales goal. Unless you want me to. If you want me to be part of that process, I can. I would prefer that you decide how you're going to generate these sales. Once you decide how you're going to do that, what you're going to do and by when, then I want you to share that with me. And as you share that with me, I'm going to have expectations regarding the results you promise.

What I did with my salespeople was negotiate expectations. We would establish up front my expectations of them in terms of handling a particular responsibility, and we'd work out their expectations of me in terms of supporting them in that direction. Leaders who do not hold employees accountable for the work they've agreed to do shortchange them in their personal growth and development.

Pinches and Crunches

Here is the idealistic situation: a salesperson's marketing efforts are perfect, and the manager gives the very best advice and support. In the real world, somewhere along the line, salespeople (and managers) do fall short. If one of my salespeople fails to perform as expected, I call it a "pinch." When pinches accumulate, when our unmet expectations are allowed to fester, they become more problematic. Eventually the accumulation of pinches will reach the explosion point, and a "crunch" will occur. This is a negative interaction caused by frustration, disappointment, and anger. Crunches damage relationships, destroy trust, and are unproductive.

As a sales manager, I know I have to deal with pinches right away if I'm to avoid crunches with salespeople. "Marty, I'm very concerned—" I assert the fact that Marty had projected what the level of sales would be by this time, and that the sales figures are lagging twenty percent behind his own and my expectations. I'll tell the salesperson that's a pinch, and I'll tell him the only thing to do is to deal with this issue right away. We need to re-project. "Why are we missing the original projections? Why do you think this is happening?"

Marty may say, "Well, I'm sorry. I made my decisions and I made my wonderful projections when we had an exclusive niche in the market. In the last three months three competitors have come out with products like ours, and their prices are fifteen percent less than ours. They are ruining our position with some of our customers. It's going to take us time to recover, so it's not going to go quite the way I thought it was going to go."

"Okay. Fine," I say, "What do you think we should do? Should we drop the product? Because we can't keep going in this direction if the sales are going down. Based on your experience, do you think that we can regain some market share?"

The salesperson replies, "Well, I can't tell you right now. Can I have a little time to think about it?"

"Sure," I reply, "Let's meet tomorrow. By tomorrow I would like to know what your decision is. If you think we should continue with the product, we can buy a little time, but you need to share with me how we're going to get this done."

The pinch has been exposed. The salesperson is asked to be accountable and still has the responsibility for getting the job done. Here the difference between caring for and caretaking someone else is apparent. I care for my salespeople, and I want to help them do their jobs. I want to support them. The caretaking manager will be satisfied with stereotyping the salesman as a loser or making the decision to drop the product himself or herself, taking care of the problem by withdrawing support. The more productive solution is to hold the person who is most able to understand the market, probably the salesperson, accountable for the next decision.

Perhaps the problem is due more to morale problems than market forces. Let's say there's a possibility that salespeople have gotten discouraged, and they're not doing what they should do. If I run the company, I go to Bill, who is the sales director. "Bill, we've got a pinch. Sales are down in this particular line. Your salespeople are charged with selling it. What's happening, in your opinion?"

Well, Bill starts telling me the same story. "Our people are out there calling on their key customers. But the new competitors are making inroads. Their price is less than ours. Quite frankly, the quality of their product is nowhere near ours. But you know how it is today. People sometimes go with price. My gut feeling says we should hang in there and continue our relationship with these customers. When they start getting complaints from their customers about the quality, I have a feeling we'll be able to get back in even more solid than before. But yes, my salespeople are making the calls. They're building relationships with the customers. Right now we have a certain number of customers who are buying at price only."

Bill, in this case, is held accountable just as his salespeople are held accountable; it's their decision what the next move should be. Working within target dates, sales quotas, activity levels, and all the rest of output measurements are fine if seen for what they are: theory, pure and simple. They don't measure long-term relationships, the referral factor, the reasons customers are loyal, or why employees do more than the minimum. It's not that what is important can't be measured, but the measure itself has to be important.

I believe salespeople who understand their customers' needs and have the creativity and resourcefulness to match the company's product or service to those needs will end up with far more sales. But it takes more than mere activity to establish that customer rapport. How do you measure the value of relationships? Look to employee morale, customers' attitudes, and the resilience of the company in the face of crises and inevitable changes. Healthy relationships survive and prosper. If you believe your business is prone to change, you should do everything possible to build a solid foundation of interpersonal relationships within the business and with your customers.

People respond when they are reinforced, when they are acknowledged for successfully meeting expectations. This is largely how we all gain confidence and grow. It is also true that when we avoid responsibility or consequences for our decisions and actions, we tend to end up in distress. We're insecure. We feel forced to play a role, hide the truth, make up excuses. The leader who can help employees be accountable is cultivating stronger, healthier employees. The manager that pulls out the whip to punish salespeople or any other employee into more effort will likely be dealing with low moods, resentment, and even poorer performance.

Understand Moods

If I told you I had the answers to all the management ills of every company in America, what would that be worth? My answer is simple: it's moods. Most companies don't talk about moods, but they should. Anyone who expects to be a leader should want to talk about moods because moods as well as values affect both attitudes and performance.

A primary responsibility of leaders is to keep oneself and others in a decision-making mode. As a custodian of morale, no responsibility has greater influence on productivity. If you are in management, you must understand your moods and how your moods affect your relationships with others. Understanding that moods are normal indicates high emotional intelligence. When people are in a low mood, their thinking is impaired, and they don't make very good decisions. If you're going to make good decisions quickly, you should first understand that even the most competent, best person you will ever work with will be in a low mood on occasion. How you deal with that situation will determine your long-term relationship with that person.

The oceans have tides; the Earth has weather, and people have moods. You may not understand them, but you know they're there, and you must acknowledge the state. You may not be able to do anything about the tides or the weather or yours or another's low mood. You can pull up the beach chairs at high tide or get out an umbrella if it's raining. And you can be sensitive to your own mood and others' moods. In most cases time will pass and the low mood will also pass. Unfortunately, sometimes we complicate and extend the problem because we continue to try and function in spite of our low mood. Denying moodiness doesn't make it go away.

Most people don't understand moods. It seems that often in the competitive business environment acknowledging a "low mood" is the same as admitting a handicap, which may put you at a disadvantage and is therefore ignored. In organizations from retail to manufacturing to civil service to nonprofits, the pressure to perform at maximum levels all the time not only has led to burnout, but in some cases to sabotage or suicide. As we begin to understand moods better, we will develop more compassion, which will enable us to build more effective relationships.

Remember your own low moods? Remember a time you accused someone or something else for what turned out to be your fault? Your low mood made you look for scapegoats. It made you feel sorry for yourself. It made you think weak thoughts. What happens when somebody else, such as one of your employees, gets in a low mood? It's easy to get in an argument with them. Haven't you seen someone behaving very badly, and you just know that they have no self-confidence, and have very low self-esteem?

The best way to deal with the indisputable fact of moods is to understand that, when you're in a low mood, you shouldn't be making critical decisions. Don't have significant interaction with subordinates. When you're in a low mood, you're likely to say things you really don't mean, and you can be very hurtful. You're apt to make decisions based on too little information, usually negative, because this is the way you feel. You're not likely to be creative because you're not relaxed.

People are relieved when someone admits that moods are normal. When in a low mood, back off from a lot of interaction with others. Focus on your work, and then just try to keep a quiet mind and relax, because the mood will go away. It will go away, and you will go to another level.

You will feel better, and then you can make better decisions and interact more effectively.

Like you, when employees are in a low mood, they're probably not feeling good about themselves or their situation. If you sense that an employee is feeling low, just say, "You know what, things aren't going too well for you today, are they? I have times like that, too. We have a picnic table out there in back, why don't I buy you a can of pop, and you go out there and relax a little bit—take a break."

I'm not suggesting you ignore performance, but perhaps temper your expectations for perfection with more compassion. Compassion is reality based, whereas expectations of perfection are arbitrary and unattainable. As a leader, you need to help that other person be more effective, to function better, and you should know it won't happen if he or she is in a low mood. It is unreasonable to expect people, including yourself, to operate at maximum efficiency and make top-quality decisions all the time.

The more flexible you can be in your business relationships, family, and social relationships, the more people will want to work with you. We're back to talking about how people integrate what their values are on and off the job. We're talking about blending. We are not talking about being soft, mushy, and permissive. We're talking about bottom-line productivity, acknowledging what is truly unproductive: insensitive, unrealistic expectations of perfection. The manager who says, "I can tough it out, I'm at peak performance level all the time, do as I do," is out of touch. This pose isn't respected; it's resented.

Most managers have never been trained to understand moods, and I'm referring to their own moods, the moods of the people that they report to, and the moods of their employees. When moods seem to take on a life of their own and begin to generalize to a lot of people, they become morale. Employee morale, manager morale, or even customer morale, they're all the same embodiment of a prevalent mood. Every organization has morale, just as every person has a mood. If a manager was taught that he or she has moods and it's normal to have both high and low moods, we'd go a long way toward better decision making.

In a corporate or business setting, we're usually encouraged to leave our moods at home. Businesses usually do not want to deal with mood or morale problems. The only problem with that is we cannot leave our moods at home. Acknowledge moods in the workplace or don't acknowledge them; they're still there. Acknowledging the constant presence and importance of morale issues, however, leads to less rigid expectations for yourself and helps people who are supposed to support other people to be less demanding of perfect roles.

Leadership

I have not read or heard about anyone promoting the dictatorial style of management, so why do so many managers adopt this style? Many people point out its short-comings, its tendency to create dependency, and its insensitivity. No manager that I know would try and justify treating employees like peons, but that's what they do. In my view, this kind of arbitrary behavior is not calculated, controlled behavior; it's probably more due to the way the manager feels. Some bosses suffer under the delusion that no one else can detect when they are in a low mood. Ordering people around, especially when you feel low, does not usually result in cooperation, but merely begrudging compliance. You may intimidate people enough to get by, but no one will mistake you for a leader. When people are made to do things, they don't feel responsible for their work, they're not invested, and they probably won't produce their best work.

The kind of authority that establishes trust and cooperation always comes from the people who are managed, the employees. An aide once asked General Dwight D. Eisenhower how he got people to do things. Ike reportedly pulled a string out of his pocket and laid it on the table. "There's only one way to get this string across the table," he began, "and it's not by pushing." After pushing it around, he proceeded to pick up one end and drag it forward. "This is how you lead people."

People do things for their own reasons, not necessarily yours. Therefore, their moods and their values should be extremely important to the leader. Knowing what causes low moods provides an insight into how to improve the quality of relationships and increase the positiveness of morale in general. Many low moods are caused by stressful situations quite common in everyday business life.

Getting someone to do anything differently involves change, and change is often stressful. At whatever level, decision making is always influenced by people's tolerance for change. It is necessary to leave something behind as you more toward something different. We must go through a grieving process, especially if it's a big decision that affects sensitive issues. From denial to anger to bargaining, depression, and finally acceptance, our emotional acceptance of a decision can lag behind our understanding of the issues that influence our decisions.

If you put the key in the ignition of a car and turn it, and it only makes a click, you know there's something wrong, maybe a dead battery. Then we turn the key and hear that click maybe two, three, or six times more. This is called denial. Then you get angry, maybe try to punish that ignition switch a little, utter a few choice epithets, slam a door. Then you start to bargain. "Oh please start, I'll get a tune-up, I'll get a new battery, but just get me to work on time!" Then there's the depression stage, the feeling sorry for yourself stage. But finally, there's acceptance. You ask a neighbor for a lift or call a tow truck.

Now, if you were on the way to the store for milk, this may be a mild inconvenience. Even though no one likes an unreliable car, it's a different matter if a dead battery threatened your job! Suppose your biggest client was waiting at the airport between flights? Suppose your third-grader was waiting to be picked up on a cold winter night. The anxiety is magnified. Depending on what the decision involves, the whole company may have to expect some grieving. Collective denial, collective anger, bargaining, depression, and finally acceptance are facts of corporate life, just as with individuals.

Leadership is a synonym for managing change and for empowering those you lead to make good decisions. With most decisions, there's bound to be a little anger and denial at first, a little resentment. Your employees might come back and try to bargain a little bit. "Can we go back to the way it was?"

You have to say "No," and some employees may leave. Some may be a little depressed, and this is okay; it's not a power struggle, insubordination, or rebellion. If you and your fellow workers continue communicating, in a relatively short period of time everyone will accept the decision. That's when you (collectively) can move on to the next decision.

These things are normal, they're expected, and the more the decision affects what's near and dear to people, the more you need to give people time to go through the stages. All the resistance, all the anger, the name calling, even bitterness is all part of grieving. You have to be sensitive to this process, or you'll really miss the boat. But if you remain in one stage too long, that's not healthy either. A good leader wants to get people to the "awareness" state without delay. That's the leader's role—to understand the grieving process and help people get through it as quickly as possible so that they can move to the next decision, which involves the next change. This is leadership—to pull other people through the process, just like Eisenhower's string.

The Outstanding Group

➤ **Collaboration means each member must help** new people to grow and achieve high levels of competence.

➤ **With trust, less nurturing of relationships is required.** Build high-intimacy/low-maintenance relationships.

➤ **Outstanding groups use the informational intelligence,** creativity, and problem-solving capabilities of individuals to meet present and future challenges.

Chapter Ten
The Outstanding Group

THE TRADITIONAL MODEL of the company has been hierarchical, top-down, with many levels of management. For years the lock-step rules and traditions in business were seen as the price of success. Go along, get along, move up, move ahead. But companies are being forced to do things differently today, if only because the top has become so crowded and unproductive. Some people have such antipathy for this kind of organizational ritual that they prefer not to participate in business at all, assuming all businesses are political pyramids. Layers of management emphasize upward mobility—the ladder of success as the goal of working. This near obsession with individual achievement often comes at the expense of colleagues, clients, and ultimately one's own peace of mind.

Collaboration

The survival of the fittest mentality is rapidly disappearing as companies flatten out, eliminate middle management and empower lower levels of decision making. Companies such as IBM, 3M, Rubbermaid, and Watkin's Products illustrate this trend. They are really imitating smaller companies, trying to capitalize on the way smaller companies use their human resources. Smaller companies have few institutionalized departmental empires and can't afford the layers of associates and assistant leaders the large corporations produce. With fewer employees, each employee is more important and has more real influence over the company's direction.

I have a client who has an eagle as a corporate logo, and after talking so much about my ideas on how people should be wingin' it as a response to rapid change, it seemed natural to tie the two themes, the eagle and the wingin' it attitude, together for a speech I was to give at the client's regional meeting. I had a hard time with the idea, however, because I don't identify success in business as the result of solo activity. I didn't use the eagle metaphor in the speech.

I have nothing against eagles or the symbolism of being the best, as long as you're talking about being the best you can be. Rather than soaring above, as master of the universe, however, I think people must share more, learn more from each other, and think more about how they can contribute more to the group. I admire stars; I can understand the inspiration they can cause, but I don't think most organizations can survive by elevating a few people to star status and ignoring the thousands of others who don't share the limelight. This is one of the weaknesses of the American preoccupation with the biggest, the bestest, and the mostest.

Groups are more productive if they can marshal collaboration, mutual support, and synergy than if they exist only to be vehicles for a competitive contest to produce an individual star performer. I see productivity increasing when all resources are shared, not when some resources are sacrificed in order to produce a winner. Perhaps the metaphor of the goose, or better, the gaggle of geese best represents the outstanding group concept. When migrating south, geese in flight take turns being the leader, while each bird unselfishly takes a key role in the formation. Both individual performance and performance in support of the group are goals of an outstanding group.

Even the Lone Ranger had help from Tonto (plus every townsperson who'd ever heard of his heroic deeds). Most successful people have a wide variety of relationships. They are able to blend into a group very easily, and they can let the group be in charge; they don't necessarily have to be in charge all the time. They are able to duplicate their strengths through other people. They've learned the secret of multiplication through the outstanding group concept.

The basis of the outstanding group is that people have chosen to be a part of a group. They leave part of their ego at home when they come to work. They're open to other people's perceptions and perspectives. They listen to other people and let them have input. All people in the group, including the receptionist, the secretary, the guy who cleans the warehouse, the person doing the inventory, or the truck driver, may have as good ideas as you do about the business and deserve to be listened to. They must be allowed to be part of the process of making decisions. An outstanding group is the same as a team in which all the individuals function together well.

In the outstanding group strong personalities are willing to tone down their competitive instincts to dominate. In some cases, the group encourages individuals who ordinarily defer to others to come out of their shell a little bit. It's an interactive process that fosters mutual respect. Everybody has an opportunity to say what they feel, and the goals of personal and company growth are primary. This is collaboration rather than competition.

The outstanding group concept supports outstanding people working together. You're allowed to reassess who you really are. Unfortunately, even though I believe you are born with a healthy self-concept and self-esteem, slowly this self-confidence can be eroded as you respond to the image of what other people expect you should be. In business, government, and many other organizations it has been assumed that everyone needs to be managed. We have expected employees to follow directions, go through channels, obey the chain of command, and just do their jobs. This uniformity requires compliance, which tends to stifle creativity and individuality. This sacrifices potential productivity for maintaining the status quo.

The trend toward encouraging autonomous groups and site-based management challenges the idea that consistency and compliance make people more productive. Clothes on the job help to illustrate this point. Everyone knows that at IBM, the blue suit, white shirt, and blue tie were the standard uniform. At IBM today, this code is now relaxed. Bill Gates, recently named by *Forbes* magazine the richest man in the world and head of one of the most successful high-tech companies, Microsoft, rarely wears a tie. The Apple revolution, starting with a couple of blue-jeaned guys in a garage has successfully challenged Big Blue.

Of course, I'm not saying you must dress casually to be successful, but it is part of a turn toward what's really important on the job. If I'm comfortable, I think better. If I'm comfortable, I have a better opportunity of reassessing who I am. If I dress according to how you want me to, I'm more liable to start thinking the way you want me to, and that's not good for me and it's not good for you. Today most employers need and expect more from employees than just doing what they're told.

Blair Witt's Story

Blair Witt is a relationship builder. He builds high intimacy relationships by the way he conducts himself, by example. By high-intimacy, I mean "trusting communication" as in the original Greek and Latin derivations, from *intimus,* meaning intrinsic, essential, and bringing in the concepts of friendship, closeness, and warmth.

Blair Witt is about six feet tall, has brown hair, and looks all-American. He's an unassuming guy. When you talk, he kind of leans toward you, and he gives you his full attention. He's just like a sponge soaking up what you say, another person who has the ability to direct his mind intensively, eliminating distractions or irrelevancies that diffuse communications. He responds with the kind of interest everyone hopes to receive. I met him in 1989. He was a regional manager for IDS (Investor Diversified Services) Financial Services in St. Cloud. He retired in his late forties. I can tell you IDS was real sad to see him retire in the prime of his earning years. To turn away from all that money, and I don't know how much, but hundreds of thousands of dollars could be an understatement, is remarkable in this day and age.

The turnover rate at IDS was about forty percent, but with Blair's unit the turnover was practically zero. He was supremely competent in his field. He knew all there was to know about IRAs, investment risks, estate planning, and so forth. Being so knowledgeable, he engendered a terrific amount of trust from his clients. But lots of financial experts haven't accomplished what Blair has been able to do, and the keys to his success involve both his personal style and his belief in the potential of everyone with whom he works.

Blair cultivates intimacy through his personal integrity. Intimate relationships are warm, and they're consistently open and up front. His ability to recruit, hire, and keep good people—and mold them into an outstanding group—is what led to the success of his IDS unit. I don't mean to say he didn't work with outstanding and talented individuals; in fact, he did, but it is the way he worked with these people that made them all very successful.

All of Blair's employees have chosen to buy into the group concept. They're highly supportive of one another. They share leads, they give each other references and referrals, and they'll take new people under their wings and help them to get up to speed. In some organizations there's a competitiveness, but not in Blair's group. The goal of the group is to get each individual to his or her level of competence. To some extent it's assumed the new member will be successful, that somehow it's part of everyone's job not to let them coast or fail. This unconditional acceptance does have parallels in other areas of our lives.

High-Intimacy/Low-Maintenance Relationships

You probably have some old friends you rarely see. Perhaps you had a best friend growing up, a neighbor, a grade school or high school buddy. Maybe you had a roommate long ago. When you see this person, though you're separated by years and miles, there is instant acceptance, instant friendship. It doesn't matter what the person's done, where they've been, or how much they earn, the bond is there, and that's what I call high intimacy. Low maintenance refers to the depth of trust which doesn't require proof or re-proof. It's what family ties are about, or the space that can be transcended in an instant but doesn't need constant cultivation. The kind of trust a good leader can engender is due both to his or her personal integrity and his or her reliance on the potential competencies of the group.

With the outstanding group concept people can reassess who they really are and can contribute to the success of the group. This democratic, self-affirming attitude makes people happier, prouder, and more productive. It is the outstanding group that uses each member's contributions to be all it can be.

Diversity in the workplace means much more than having a mix of people from various cultures, races, or ethnic origins on the payroll. The fact that people appear different from one another or talk differently is a superficial sign of diversity. Diversity describes the richness, the depth, and the balances that occur with a mixture of strong individuals whose differences are complementary. The way we work in a diverse group can produce chaos or it can produce outstanding results. The difference depends upon how relationships are cultivated.

Diverse groups can be very strong. It's very similar to diversity in nature. A diverse ecosystem not only looks varied, but its balanced composition and interaction mean it is a stronger environment. The monoculture environment is susceptible to blight and devastation, vulnerable to its own weaknesses, whereas the diverse culture thrives. This metaphor emphasizes more than the aesthetics of color and variety, and this is an important emphasis, because often diversity as a business issue is relegated to "wouldn't it be nice" kinds of social engineering platitudes.

Diversity in our businesses could mean our survival, and I believe that a monocultural workplace that may have survived in the past will not in the future. Rather than monopolizing a market by controlling a particular product or service like the old AT&T, IBM, and the American automobile companies, all companies today face competition from other companies, big and small, domestic and foreign. Not only do we face competition from other businesses, but we must accommodate a customer market which is more diverse and tougher to please. With the global economy, mass marketing has changed because diverse customers demand customized treatment. We must rely upon field intelligence to direct our research, development, and marketing efforts in order to stay on top of our vast markets.

All employees must pull their weight in providing the kind of intelligence that companies must have to make good decisions. Companies who respect this aspect of their employees' value and who encourage individual contributions will prosper. Continuous improvement means constantly reengineering, anticipating constant change, and including everyone in the company's commitment to its own growth and development. Those that can make groups of achievement-oriented individuals perform in concert with one another will grow even faster. When I see companies fostering individual growth, and I see employees encouraged at all levels to be creative and do more than they get paid to do, I have renewed faith that we're headed in the right direction.

Leaders in companies can establish high-intimacy/low-maintenance relationships with all employees. The power of values that have been communicated to everyone extends beyond the present. All new hires are influenced by the adopted culture, and constant reinforcement of these values in action keeps everyone clued into what the company thinks is important. This climate provides opportunities for individuals to perform at high levels. Outstanding groups operate more by culture than coercion, more by self-motivation than mandate, and more by shared values than rules. People who work with other people should pay attention to others' needs. The quality and character of relationships within groups influence both individual and group performance.

Embrace Challenge

Does this work in large companies? Can you incorporate these ideas in a system that may not be functioning all that well to begin with? Can outstanding groups be created out of existing resources? Yes.

Two managers at Hewlett-Packard, Mei-Lin Cheng and Julie Anderson, were charged with reengineering a shipping process that had been identified as disastrously slow. It was taking twenty-six days from order to delivery for a product to reach the customer. Hewlett-Packard, a multi-billion-dollar company known for high-tech systems, had to fix this problem. A recent article in *Fortune* titled "Secrets of HP's 'Muddled' Team" featured their story.

These managers' approach to the problem began with a bargain they struck with their bosses. They promised to produce "significant and measurable improvements in customer satisfaction" in less than nine months, or their funding would disappear. They were given freedom to accomplish the goals in any way they could, and they in turn gave this freedom to a group of thirty-five people from HP and two other companies. They refused to tell anyone what to do. They used their leadership skills to tap into the emotional intelligence of the people in the group. They forced the group to adopt the receiver mode. The result was that they hit all of their measurable goals—in eight months—but they proved much more.

The first thing Anderson and Cheng did was to remove titles, calling cards, hierarchy, and step-by-step milestones of progress. Of course, complete chaos resulted, but they held to their "no plan." After the members spent a few weeks experiencing all phases of the present product delivery, they were told to start. "Start what? Start where?" The anxiety level was high.

"Just start. Come up with some answers. You are just as smart as anyone else in figuring out these problems."

The team struggled with this process. They wanted to implement a design, solve the problems, but no one would tell them what they should do. Cheng and Anderson admit they resisted the temptation to suggest solutions they thought might be best; had they "taken over," this would have doomed the process. The resulting process of creativity and innovation hooked the participants into giving their best and creating solutions themselves. They experimented. They re-designed. They tried new things. Bit by bit they practiced trying something, evaluated its practicality, and altered their solutions accordingly. They all reported that they felt they were thrown into the water over their heads, yet the collective intelligence of the team slowly began to create solutions. Ideas would come "spontaneously."

Group members, including the managers, came to realize that no individuals had all the answers. They realized that the resources of the group were greater than any individual. The article suggested that this approach could be called "management by getting out of the way." The potential of organizing this kind of outstanding group exists everywhere people work together.

Many companies shudder at the prospect of team decision making. First, the potential for interpersonal conflict increases the more teams are encouraged. Second, in the past, team decision making has meant approval by committee. Both of these concepts are not what today's outstanding groups are designed to produce. In the first instance, cooperation obviates many of the conflicts that arise when the group is designed as a contest for individuals. The outstanding group will not tolerate an arrogant or manipulative member. The second fear misunderstands the essence of the group concept. The outstanding group is not charged with approving or disapproving anything; the mandate is to act upon the situation presented to it. It's a challenge to problem solve, create a remedy, produce an effect. This is a decision-making body, not a bureaucratic exercise.

At some point successful companies realize that what they have done in the past will not last. They figure they must stay ahead of the curve. They must begin to create their future business today. This is analogous to what individuals must also do, namely, to prepare for tomorrow's work today. But for companies, this requires mobilizing a lot of people to work on what might happen in the future. Many labor forces are not interested, are not encouraged, and may be incapable of such participation.

However, I believe, if given the chance and the leadership, every company is capable of marshaling present employees' expertise to look into the future, to see the possibilities and opportunities. Market research and forecasting are the twin mantras of nineties sales success. The outstanding group will utilize the intelligence (information) of everyone who engineers, makes, sells, and delivers products and services to the customer. Obtaining and using the information company that employees possess should be a top priority, and groups organized around the outstanding group concept will be able to share this critical data. Consulting firms specializing in this kind of research call it continuous feedback. They encourage all kinds of surveying tools, assessment instruments, and longitudinal statistical measures to quantify feedback. I think it is critical to use the information that employees are privy to, but it's not the kind of information likely to appear on a computerized response sheet.

Empowering individuals and groups to solve problems for the company is ultimately the best use of people because it acknowledges what people have that machines don't—imagination. People can multiply their output if motivated to do so—machines can't. Employees know from their thousands of interactions and experiences with products, services, and customers what is going on—the best machines can only quantify what someone tells them is going on. People can assess what is right to do because of their ability to make judgments based on values. We have a long way to go before such complex concepts can be programmed into a chip.

Afterword

This last chapter is more than a summary of the ideas presented so far. It's a challenge to you to incorporate these ideas into your daily life. If you're wingin' it already, you have already found plenty to agree with so far, and I'd urge you to help others do what you do. If you're eager to learn more than you know now, let this discussion be a jumping-off place for you to take charge of your own self-development. The ability to make good decisions quickly has never been more important to individuals and to the companies that depend on all of us individuals.

I really like the spirit that the phrase "wingin' it" evokes. It makes me smile and raise my eyebrows just by saying it. And it reminds me of the characteristics of vitality and boldness that successful decision makers have in great supply. I also know that some people wince at the idea of wingin' it because they associate this expression with rash, uninformed, seat-of-the-pants decision making. I regret that this expression sometimes has that connotation. Successful people rarely make careless, off-the-cuff decisions.

To improvise is probably a more formal synonym for how I use the phrase wingin' it. I believe that people should be improvising all the time, and not only in desperate situations. I think improvising all the time is productive, creative, and energizing. People who are good at improvising have lots of practice; for some it becomes a wonderful way of life. Successful improvisation requires discipline. Two components must be achieved for successful improvisation: quick decision making, and good decision making; both quick and good, either criteria alone is not good enough.

Many successful people have achieved fame, fortune, health, and happiness by wingin' it. All of them rely upon their self-confidence, their own resources for positive values, and their ability to apply available information to make things happen. All over the country, one of the greatest problems corporate leaders have is that, even when they do have positive values and they are informed, they can't seem to make decisions quickly, and they and their companies suffer because of it. They may know a lot, but they fail to act, or they fail to act soon enough.

Anyone can learn or relearn to improvise, but it takes more than knowledge. Quick decision making can be practiced and perfected if you can reduce the risks of being wrong or criticized, and this is why I believe that clarifying and prioritizing values is so important. You will never be wrong if your decisions can be backed by your and the company's values. Management's responsibility to help you make better decisions more quickly presupposes you will not be criticized for doing what you think is best. There is no doubt in my mind that people who can improvise are happier and more successful. They attract other successful people to work with them.

I'll be talking to people about wingin' it, and someone will look at me and say, "That's common sense."

I reply, "Yes, it is. But in your life is it common practice?"

"No."

"Why is that?"

"Well, you know, you don't have the situations I have to deal with—my boss, my job, my husband, my family, and my friends. I've got all these things to deal with and it's just not that easy to make decisions. You have no idea what I've got to deal with."

And I say, "Yes, I do. There are people and there are circumstances and there are situations. And the question is, how do you choose to deal with those situations? You're not going to change those people, your boss, and most circumstances in life. But you can decide for yourself how you relate to them. Do they control you or do you control you?"

I like the empowering feeling I get from Charles Swindoll's poem "Attitude." He writes, "We cannot change our past; we cannot change the fact that people will act in a certain way. We cannot change the inevitable. The only thing we can do is play on the string we have, and that is our attitude."

Most people would probably feel more secure if everything happened according to their plan. When I was a corporate executive for years I did strategic planning. We decided revenue projections. We knew which product or how much of the product of this category we were going to sell, and what the margin was going to be. I was an expert planner!

In the late eighties, it just didn't work any more. Our competitors were lowering their prices. They were making stuff just as good as we were, but selling it for less. Our projections went out the window. Our salespeople would say, "Hey, it isn't working! Your planning and our sales don't figure!" And I didn't have any other way to set goals for our salespeople. I now know from reading the business magazines and business books that my situation is not uncommon at all today. What I find appealing about the concept of wingin' it is that it always allows for the possibility of responding to new learning with new decisions. With more global competition, we have trouble predicting where we'll be next month, never mind ten years from now. This whole book is about how we can make good decisions more quickly.

I believe we must go with the moment. If you're faced with a problem, make the very best decision you can make at that particular moment based upon your feelings and understanding of your business. At least make the best decision you can with the information you have. If you call a committee meeting and sit down and analyze the problem for three months, your competitor will eat your lunch. Speed is a prerequisite for competitive success.

Consequences for not making decisions quickly include missed opportunities, disappointment, and sometimes terminal failure. Unfortunately, not deciding is making a decision by default, and it carries consequences. Refusing to make decisions is also usually a factor of resisting change. To decide, after all, is to initiate a change.

Unfortunately, darn little advice is out there to help people make better and quicker decisions that can stand up in today's business environment. We now have access to more information than ever before in the history of mankind, and this rate of information explosion will only accelerate as information and communication technologies expand.

Conventional wisdom in problem solving and decision making has held that by identifying the problem, assembling all available information, making two columns, one pro and one con, seeking out everything there is to know before making a decision, eventually you will be more apt to make the right decision. We all know how to make good decisions. The irony today is that we have more information, but not enough time to consider it all. We don't have time enough to consider all the information available to us for two reasons: too much competition and too many choices.

We live and work in an open marketplace driven by the instant availability of information through networked personal computers. Others have access to the same information we do. The race is to best utilize the information we have to make better decisions and gain an advantage in the competitive workplace. The advantage does not accrue to the decision maker who can amass the most information, but to the person who can make the right decision in the least amount of time. The success of the person who can improvise depends upon being able to use available information. Reliance upon the information itself is devalued, in favor of using the decision maker's intuition, maturity, experience, and willingness to take a relative risk in deciding with limited or incomplete information.

People who improvise know they are taking risks, but they also have the confidence in knowing what they want to achieve. This knowledge is based on inner values as much as future goals. The best decisions are based on emotional intelligence.

Having choices from which to select solutions and having the luxury of time to weigh all factors greatly reduce the stress we all feel in making decisions. But both of these conditions may be in short supply today. A person who is wingin' it is focused on moving ahead, thinking about how decisions will affect business down the road (not up the ladder). This self-reliant person makes quick decisions because the goal is clear and the choices are narrowed by his or her own sense of values.

Speed of decision making, although essential for a competitive advantage in business, has little to do with the quality of the decisions made. This is an important lesson to learn for those who doubt the quality of decisions just because they were made quickly. A person with a positive attitude can act quickly, accept change, and will be more competitive in a changing environment. What determines the quality of decisions are sound values and good information.

For most of the industrial age, business cycles, marketing campaigns, and the way the work force was organized were fairly stable. We're experiencing radical product, marketing, and organizational change—ready or not. The era when you could come out with a new widget, a new idea, or new concept and have it exclusively for a period of time to make the big killing is pretty well dead. It's gone. Why? Profitability.

You've got two ways to go today in this global marketplace. You can go with a commodity, which is basically price: "We've got a good idea, we're pricing it low, and we'll sell a whole jillion of these at this price."

Or you can go with relationships, which means: "We're in business for the long haul; we're building effective relationships with our customers, giving them a good product and service, and we'll sell on the basis of our value, not at the lowest price." Your daily decision making, which is how you do your business, is infinitely easier with the relationships model.

For one thing, you don't have to comparison shop. You don't have to figure percentages of this to get under that to steal this market share. You make decisions based on customer relationships, your long-term commitment to the customer's satisfaction, and your standard for quality. As my friend and super salesman Tom Winninger maintains, "Understanding what your customers can afford, controlling costs and quality on your end, and being consistently fair will insure you a competitive price and a repeat customer."

A solid core of personal values and a high level of emotional intelligence are two characteristics of people who make better decisions and make intimate working relationships.

We have the potential to be more than we are. Have the confidence to invest in yourself. Have the confidence to invest in other people.

Take that confidence to work with you.

To order additional copies of this book,
please send full amount plus $4.00 for
postage and handling for the first book and
50¢ for each additional book.

Send orders to:

Galde Press, Inc.
PO Box 460
Lakeville, Minnesota 55044-0460

Credit card orders call 1–800–777–3454
Phone (612) 891-5991 • Fax (612) 891-6091
Visit our web site at http://www.galdepress.com

Write for our free catalog.

The author is available for
seminars and workshops.